GOING NATIVE IN TENERIFE

NativeSpain.™.com

GOING NATIVE IN TENERIFE

Andrea & Jack Montgomery

NativeSpain™*.com*

First Published in Great Britain 2009 by www.BookShaker.com

Typeset in Trebuchet

DISCLAIMER
While all attempts have been made to verify information provided in this publication, neither the Author nor the Publisher assumes any responsibility for errors, inaccuracies or omissions. Any slights of people or organisations are unintentional. The purchaser or reader of this publication assumes responsibility for the use of these materials and information.

Praise for this book

"Fantastic for those who want to experience that little bit extra from Tenerife, informative and precise without over kill."

Sean Coward, Director Living Tenerife Magazine
"Full of insights, wit and charm, this is the ideal companion as you explore and unlock the secrets of the real Tenerife."

Leslie Beeson, author 'Tenerife Lifeline'
"Witty and jam-packed with useful information, Going Native in Tenerife is an invaluable resource. A must for anyone thinking of visiting the island."

John Beckley, Managing Director, Sorted Sites
"Amazingly accurate observations, written in the authors' typically witty style. A highly accurate snapshot of the real Tenerife, which is sure to seduce tourists looking for things to do other than just sunbathe."

Chris Shaw, Director, Pink Elephant PR.
"What a wonderful insight into Tenerife. Written with passion, great knowledge and a love of all things Tinerfeño. A real insider's guide to the hidden treasures of this fascinating Island."

Robert and Linda Howe, visitors to Tenerife

Contents

Overview

INTRODUCTION

Tenerife is an island that attracts over 6 million visitors a year, many of whom believe they know it like the back of their hands and few of whom know it at all.

Sitting 1300 km south of mainland Spain and 300 km off the coast of West Africa in the middle of the seven major islands that make up the Canarian Archipelago, Tenerife is the most populous and one time capital of the Canary Islands.

It was created by volcanic eruptions between 7 and 12 million years ago and after Hawaii, is the highest volcanic island on the planet, rising to 3718 metres at the magnificent peak of Mount Teide; Spain's highest mountain, the globe's third highest volcano and enduring symbol of the island.

Shaped like an anvil, the island measures just 56 km at its widest point and 86 km in length and is home to a population of 865,000 (2007), 42% of whom live in the capital city of Santa Cruz or the former capital of La Laguna.

Over 40% of Tenerife's surface is protected by special measures; the centre of the island at 2000 metres and above is occupied by the volcanic wonderland of Teide National Park, a UNESCO World Heritage Site. Below that, a crown of dense pine forest known as *Corona Forestal* National Park circles the peak. In the northern mountains of Anaga, rare laurel forests from the earth's tertiary era still thrive, survivors of the ice age. Throughout the island, steep *barrancos* (ravines) cut into the cliffs are home to many of the 140 exclusive species of indigenous flora and make up some of the 107 areas of special interest.

The ratio of land mass (2034 km²) to height gives Tenerife a range of terrain and microclimates that take you through arid alpine, tropical, sub-tropical and semi-desert. In winter, you can throw snowballs in the Teide National Park and then sunbathe on the coast within just an hour's journey by car. It can be quite a bizarre sight to see a car arrive at the hot, sunny coast with a partially melted snowman riding the bonnet.

In the far west of the island, you can drive through a tunnel and emerge in an entirely different climatic zone, sometimes moving from dense cloud to unbroken blue skies. Walking its myriad of paths enables you to clearly see and feel changes in vegetation and air temperature as you cross climate zones from humid to arid and from coast to pine forest.

Tenerife is an Island of Contrasts

Step back from the coastal resorts and you're stepping back in time to a way of life that still holds family values as closely as it holds its Catholic beliefs; where Lent begins with the wild exuberance of Carnaval; where Easter is the most sacred and solemn of holidays; where Sundays are for mass and for spending with family and where the Church is a part of everyday life and its plaza the venue for evening socialising and local fiestas.

Away from the resorts too, very few people speak any English at all and there are sparse concessions to tourism, even though it's now the Island's number one income generator. Life in rural communities is hard; narrow terraces still have to be tilled by hand and younger generations are seeking easier ways of making money by heading to the coastal tourist towns. As a result, many terraces are left to go fallow, adding dry brush to fuel the not uncommon forest fires.

For an island that so many people think they know, the vast majority of it bears no resemblance to the mock Las Vegas look, designer label shops and man made beaches of the coastal resorts.

While Playa de Las Américas invests millions of euros in five star hotels themed on traditional Tenerife villages, in the Anaga Mountains life in the real thing remains much the same as it has done for centuries. Back breaking farming is a way of life; the flashing neon temperature sign outside the *farmacia* is what passes for disco lights and people still live in caves, albeit ones that now have satellite TV.

And it's just as likely that the folks who live in Roque Bermejo and Taganana know as little about the southern resorts, as the millions of visitors who annually flock there, know about them.

A BRIEF HISTORY

Up until the late 15th century, the island of Tenerife was still in the Stone Age.

It was populated by the Guanche; tribes of primitive people who dressed in animal skins, lived in caves and survived by fishing, livestock-rearing and subsistence farming. Having no naturally occurring metals on the island, the Guanche never progressed beyond wood and stone as their implements and weapons.

Despite their elemental appearance and abodes, the Guanche had an ordered social structure based around nine kingdoms *(menceyates)* each ruled by a King (*Mencey*) and a sophisticated embalming process for their dead. Many Guanche mummies have been discovered buried in caves on the island and the best preserved are on show in the Museum of Man and Nature in Santa Cruz.

The origins of the tall, fair skinned and strong Guanche is a source of controversy on the Island. It's generally accepted that they originated from the Berber tribes of North Africa but, possessing no boat building skills, there's speculation and disagreement as to how they got here; 300 kilometres is an awfully long way to swim.

In 1494, the ambitious Spaniard Alonso Fernández de Lugo raised enough finance from private investors to gather together an invading army and landed at Santa Cruz where he officially founded the city. He marched his troops westwards to take Taoro, the most powerful of the island's Menceys.

Passing through a deep *barranco* (ravine) at Acentejo, he was ambushed by the Guanche with their stones and spears and his army was decimated. He barely escaped with his life. Today, the site of the battle is known as La Matanza – the massacre.

The following year de Lugo returned and on flat ground more suited to the Spanish crossbows, he defeated the Guanche at Aguere near La Laguna and again further along the Acentejo barranco at what today is known as La Victoria.

In 1496 de Lugo completed the conquest of Tenerife on behalf of the Crown of Castille and made himself *Adelantado* or first governor of the island.

Under de Lugo's auspices, much of the north of the island was given to wealthy Genoese, Portuguese and Spanish merchants in return for their financing of the conquest and with the proviso that they plant sugar cane. The cane grew well in Tenerife's climate and throughout the 16th century the island became wealthy on its proceeds until production in the Antilles and Brazil undercut it and the trade began to falter.

Tenerife's development was taking place at the same time as the world map was being re-drawn. Columbus had sailed past Tenerife on his voyage of 1492, unable to land due to the savages who inhabited the, as yet unconquered, island. With the discovery of the New World came a vast new trading market for which Tenerife was perfectly placed as the stepping stone between Europe and the Americas. In a frontier society where silk, spices, gold, fine art and slaves were being exchanged, fortunes were out to be made...and stolen, and Tenerife became a magnet for merchants, artisans, clerical orders, nobility and pirates.

This influx of foreign money and influence is reflected in the architecture of Santa Cruz, La Laguna and La Orotava where the wealthiest of the settlers made their homes.

When the sugar trade began to collapse, vines replaced the canes and wine production brought wealth throughout the 17th and most of the 18th centuries, particularly for the La Orotava valley where the Malvasia grape produced Malmsey wine which was considered the best in the world and the favourite tipple of Europeans.

For the little town of Garachico with its deep natural harbour, trade with the New World had brought untold riches, but all that changed in 1706 when an eruption from Montaña Negra filled the harbour with lava, destroying the town's most valuable asset. With much of Garachico buried under lava, the trade spotlight turned on the port of Orotava (Puerto de la Cruz) and to Santa Cruz where rapid expansion began to attract the attentions of the British.

In 1797, led by Admiral Horatio Nelson, English ships attempted to storm the port of Santa Cruz and steal New World gold from the *San José* which was moored there. The English were resoundingly defeated by the Santa Cruceros under the command of General Gutiérrez and Nelson lost his right arm in the battle.

The second half of the 18th century had also seen a downturn in the fortunes of Tenerife's wine trade. The European palate was changing and the new kid on the block, at a fraction of the price, was Portugal's Madeira wine. By the 19th century, Tenerife's wine trade had collapsed and the Tinerfeños left in their droves for the New World and the promise of a better life. Families setting sail from Santa Cruz founded the cities of Montevideo in Uruguay and San Antonio (site of the Alamo) in Texas and forged links with the Americas that were to shape the future of the island.

It wasn't until the late 19th century when the Frenchman Berthelot brought banana production to the island that Tenerife's fortunes revived and her landscape took on the appearance it still maintains today.

Barely had the island got back onto its economic feet when the First World War halted exports, causing widespread hardship and sending the Tinerfeños in their thousands to Cuba and Venezuela.

When, in 1936 a troublesome former Commander-in-Chief of the Spanish army was posted to Santa Cruz to take up his post as military governor of the Canary Islands, the plot to overthrow the Spanish Republican government wasn't ended, it merely re-located. In July of that year, General Francisco Franco left his offices in Santa Cruz for the shores of North Africa from where he began the offensive that would lead to the Spanish Civil War.

Timeline

- 500BC – Tenerife's first settlers mysteriously arrive from the Berber region of North Africa.
- 1392 – two Guanche shepherds find a statue of the Virgin and child on a beach in Güímar and after firstly attempting to stone her, then to knife her, they finally settle down to worship her and she has remained the object of Tinerfeños' fervent reverence to this day.
- 1494 – City of Santa Cruz founded by Alonso Fernández de Lugo who then leads his troops into an ambush and is soundly thrashed by the spears and stones of primitive warriors; Tenerife 1 – Spain 0.
- 1495 – de Lugo returns to defeat the Guanche at Aguere and then again at Acentejo; Tenerife 1 – Spain 2.
- 1496 – Conquest of Tenerife on behalf of the Crown of Castille; final whistle.
- 1519 – Fernando de Magallanes sails from Tenerife on a journey that leads to the discovery of the Magellan Straits.
- 1657 – English Admiral Robert Blake attempts to take the port of Santa Cruz and is defeated, setting a trend for the future.
- 1706 – port of Garachico destroyed by eruption of Montaña Negra and the English try once again to take Santa Cruz, this time Rear Admiral John Jennings is defeated.
- 1797 – Rear Admiral Horatio Nelson loses his right arm in the third and final unsuccessful attempt by the English to take Santa Cruz.
- 1821 – Santa Cruz awarded status of capital city of the Canary Islands.

- 1927 – Santa Cruz loses status as capital of Canary Islands; easy come...
- 1935 – André Breton officially declares Tenerife a surrealist island; a fact which comes as no surprise to anyone who's attended Carnaval.
- 1936 – General Franco is posted to Santa Cruz from where he begins the Spanish Civil War; presumably the Spanish don't know that old adage 'Keep your friends close and your enemies closer'.
- 1941 – Los Rodeos airport opens in the north of the island.
- 1978 – having spent 150 years trying to keep them out, Tenerife opens the Reina Sofia airport in the south and the British invade.
- 1983 – Canary Islands become two autonomous regions with Santa Cruz de Tenerife designated capital of the Western Isles and Las Palmas de Gran Canaria capital of the Eastern Isles.

PEOPLE AND THEIR QUIRKS

In recent times, the islanders have elevated Tenerife's original inhabitants, the Guanche to almost god like status. Towns, landmarks and hotels have Guanche names, and statues all over Tenerife are dedicated to the proud, but primitive people who populated the island pre-conquest. The irony is that the conquistadors decimated the indigenous population, so in truth islanders are more likely to be descended from the invaders and yet you'll be hard pressed to find a statue honouring non-Guanche 'heroes' of the conquest.

Some places remained Guanche strongholds after the conquest; Tacoronte, Santiago Valley; the Orotava Valley and Güímar, where physician and merchant Dr Eden recorded in 1662 about the Guanche population:

"...the poorest think themselves too good to marry with the best Spaniard."

Interestingly these areas tend to have more than their fair share of beautiful men and women; the tiny town of Santiago del Teide producing at least two Miss and one Mr Spain.

Guanche Kings at Candelaria

The nationalities of Tenerife's settlers also provide an insight into why the islanders don't primarily consider themselves Spanish. The architects, engineers, merchants and farmers who fashioned Tenerife post conquest were a mix of Spanish, Italians, Portuguese, Flemish, Irish and British; an eclectic bunch, which combined to produce the 'Tinerfeño'.

The island's slogan is appropriately *'Tenerife Amable'*; Tinerfeños are generally a good natured, generous and friendly lot. Even in the most remote villages, visitors are greeted with a smile and a *'buenos dias'*. There's none of that wary suspicion that can be encountered in some small communities. Being at the crossroads of the world for five centuries, the appearance of a stranger isn't exactly something new.

They have a laid back approach to life; 'working to live' rather than the other way around. Nothing is rushed and everything stops for the seemingly endless merry-go-round of fiestas.

Their 'easy come, easy go' outlook can occasionally be frustrating. They queue patiently for hours in the *Correos* (Post Office) and *Concorcio de Tributos* (Government utility offices) without complaining. When some nationalities, no names mentioned, try to queue jump Tinerfeños say nothing. Whilst Brits huff and puff, the Tinerfeño shrugs their shoulders, commenting: *"Tranquilo*, we'll all be served at some point."

It's an attitude which makes you feel petty, but it does perpetuate inefficient systems designed to keep Post Office and Government workers in a job, rather than having anything to do with customer service.

When Tinerfeños meet socially, conversations are lively and can sound aggressive, especially those involving dominoes or Zanga, a local card game played around harbours and plazas, but it's all just good-natured banter. Displays of anger are rare. A Canarian friend tried to describe a particularly obnoxious Englishman in his bar.

"He was so annoying... that he..." my friend searched for the right words. "...he even made a Canario angry."

Eating habits are much the same as the rest of Spain; the main meal being taken in the afternoon, followed by a siesta. Apart from those in purpose built tourist resorts and in modern shopping centres, most shops shut between 13.30 and 16.30 and even the capital, Santa Cruz, is eerily quiet during these hours.

Tinerfeños are passionate about sport and everyone supports the island's football team, CD Tenerife. The highlight of the football calendar is the home game against rivals UD Las Palmas from neighbouring Gran Canaria, which attracts a level of excitement that the arrival of Barcelona or Real Madrid couldn't match.

Bullfighting has never taken off on the island, something which locals will tell you proudly, as though it gives them the moral high ground over their mainland cousins. Santa Cruz does have a bullring, but it's used for concerts and political rallies. Tinerfeños prefer *Lucha Canario* (Canarian wrestling) which is like sumo wrestling in nappies or, as Freddie, a young Tinerfeño, describes it: "fighting without violence". Nearly every town has a wrestling ring and during the season it's primetime Saturday night viewing on local TV channels.

A good place for observing the Tinerfeño character is on the island's roads. If every male on the island lost their left arm tomorrow it wouldn't change their driving habits. The limb hangs limply out the window, never venturing inside for gear changes or to help negotiate corners. It only springs into life to acknowledge friends, or to apologise for cutting you up.

On country roads, locals drive incredibly slowly; tootling along at 30km an hour, honking their horns and waving at everyone they pass. If the first two letters of the registration of the car in front is 'TF', sit back and enjoy the scenery, you're not going anywhere in a hurry.

Every night there are public service broadcasts on TV to educate drivers about how to tackle 'new fangled' concepts like slip roads and roundabouts, where most Tinerfeños avoid the inner lane altogether. It might go against the grain, but it's safer to stay in the outside lane like everyone else.

Being an island, there is a tendency to be a little inward looking. Although Tinerfeños are welcoming towards visitors, they're less open to advice from outsiders, preferring to stick with tried and trusted, but not always successful, methods. This has contributed to a boom and bust economy which has dogged Tenerife throughout its history. On one hand tradition remains strong and there's a wonderful feeling of community everywhere; on the other development in some areas is painfully slow. Information Technology is years behind much of Europe and many businesses, and some town councils, don't have websites, despite the fact that many potential customers lie beyond the island's coastline. Although tourism has been the mainstay of the economy for forty years and millions of British descend on the island annually English isn't widely spoken outside of the resorts.

Tinerfeños have an inferiority complex in relation to mainland Spain; believing that mainlanders view the Canary Islands as being backward. It's a belief which isn't without foundation.

When godos, (a slang term for mainland Spanish) descend on the island in the summer they joke:

"You'll always be behind us...an hour behind us."

At face value it's an innocent reference to Tenerife time being on GMT whereas Spain is an hour ahead, but the fixed false grin on the Tinerfeño recipient's face tells you they know what's really being said.

THE FLAVOUR OF TENERIFE

Pre PC, the phrase, 'melting pot' was often used to describe a thriving, international metropolis such as London, New York, Paris or Hong Kong where teeming hordes of people could be expected to hail from all corners of the globe making each city a great cauldron where the individual characteristics of each culture melted together.

But like spice in the pot, the special districts of every big city - the Chinatown, or Latin Quarter, Little Italy or African market – add their own colour and flavour so something about the melting pot didn't ring true. It wasn't long before the Melting Potters were put in their place by the emergence of the Salad Bowlers.

Salad Bowlers embrace the individuality of each ingredient in the bowl and celebrate the glorious mix of colours and textures that could be found in the large cities. Far from melting together each cultural ingredient stood out to be savoured and enjoyed as a small part of the whole.

So what about Tenerife? Is it a melting pot, full of different nationalities that have homogenized themselves to become one smooth salsa or salad bowl where each national character stands out to provide a delicious dish?

Considering the eccentricities of my assorted neighbours I would have to say Tenerife is most like a bag of assorted nuts but my Galician neighbour disagrees and asserts that a large paella would be more appropriate. All flavours under the sun, complementing each other in a delicious and aromatic blend. Hmmm, okay throw in the occasional fishy whiff of timeshare scams and I might settle on that.

The thing is that from outside looking in, Tenerife is not an obviously international destination. Newcomers are often surprised by the rich cultural diversity that is to be found here. At least in the South of the island, the residents are as likely to be from anywhere other than Tenerife as they are to be Canarian. In the group of houses in my community we have Belgians, Finns, Scots, Alicante and Galicia Mainlanders, Italians, French and Columbians. The only Canarians are Santa Cruz weekenders who pop down South every second Sunday.

At a recent street party as I blethered with my neighbours it struck me that the only true Tinerfeñans present were our children. Where each of the adults had quite literally brought their own national flavour to the table by bringing along a plate of shortbread or pote gallego according to the country or state where they were born, all the kids at the party were born here in Tenerife.

They all, regardless of where their parents came from, speak fluent Spanish and use it as their group language. It is not that the kids are not aware of the national differences between them, they simply didn't care. So I guess they had the answer all along. Tenerife is like a box of chocolates. Nobody cares what's on the outside as long as the centre is sweet.

Julie Hume, Tenerife information for tourists and ex-pat residents, *www.etenerife.com*

LANGUAGE

Like so much of its culture, Tenerife's language has its roots firmly in Latin America, not in Mainland Spain.

The most immediately obvious differences are firstly, the use of the 's' sound instead of the lisped 'th'; so *'gracias'* is pronounced *'grasias'* rather than the Castilian *'grathias'* and secondly, the use of *'usted'* and *'ustedes'* to address anyone except children; in Tenerife, the term *'vosotros'* is almost considered an insult.

And some words are uniquely Canarian, for example the bus is known as the *guagua* (pronounced wah wah) as if everyone were still three years old and potatoes are *'papas'*, which is rather nice.

But these pale into insignificance when faced with the spoken word of the majority of Canarios, for it's the almost complete disregard for the letter 's' and the propensity to merge entire sentences into a single sound which confounds even the most practiced of Spanish speakers when they arrive here.

The 's' sound is dropped from the end of words, so that *'mas'* and *'menos'* become *'mah'* and *'menoh'*, and then they're run together so that the popular sentiment and accurate descriptor of Canarian life; *'mas o menos'* (more or less) becomes *'maomenoh'*.

This lax use of pronunciation can inevitably lead to confusion, particularly when used in relation to appointments when, for example 2.30 (*dos y media*) is interpreted as 12.30 (*doce y media*), the 'y' having been swallowed altogether.

Particularly confounding can be any conversation which refers to the island of La Palma or the city of Las Palmas, the capital of Gran Canaria, both being pronounced *"La' Palmah'"*. It can take five minutes to establish precisely where the action is taking place before you get to the plot.

Men are particularly prone to dropping practically all their vowel sounds and running everything together like an over zealous seamstress making comprehension virtually impossible, even amongst themselves. If you listen in to two elderly gents having a conversation, you'll find that a good proportion of it is spent in each clarifying exactly what the other is saying.

For those arriving here having invested time learning the basics of Spanish, it feels a bit like having been taught English and then dropped in Glasgow or Newcastle; you wonder if there are actually two languages called Spanish and you've just learned the wrong one.

You can enrol full or part time at any of the proliferation of language schools on the island or at the University of La Laguna where, for a price, you can move from unconsciously incompetent to consciously incompetent and stay there for quite some time. On the plus side, mumbling over uncertain verb endings will rarely be interpreted as incompetence and can even heighten comprehension. In any case, they'll smile warmly, tell you your Spanish is '*muy bueno*' and continue to chat endlessly to you as if you're taking in every word. Just throw in the occasional '*claro*', '*vale*' and '*venga*' and they'll never know the difference.

CULTURE

It has been said in the past that Tenerife has less culture than the average pot of yoghurt and if you were to ask anyone to name someone famous who comes from Tenerife, they'd struggle. Famous writers, poets, musicians, there've been a few, but in the words of Frank Sinatra, "but then again, too few to mention."

Auditorio de Tenerife - Santa Cruz

Some claim to fame can go to the island's Surrealist connection when, back in 1937, after hosting the second Universal Surrealism Exhibition, André Breton signed a manifesto declaring Tenerife a 'Surrealist Island'. La Laguna-born Oscar Dominguez painted alongside Breton in Paris and his 1937 oil painting "The Infernal Machine" fetched a record breaking FF2,770,000 in Paris in 2000. The front door to Dominguez' birthplace in La Laguna is framed by a large sardine can with the lid rolled open...very surreal.

The Teatro Güimerá in Santa Cruz is named after the Tenerife-born playwright Angél Güimerá and was opened in 1851, becoming an obligatory venue for every Spanish theatre company en route to touring the Americas. It's a typical nineteenth century bourgeois theatre, all gold leaf and frescoes, and today continues to stage theatre and ballet.

Several small towns on the island also have theatres which stage surprisingly professional performances; El Sauzal and Arico come particularly to mind.

But the event that really put the yoghurt joke to rest was the opening of Santiago Calatrava's spectacular Auditorio de Tenerife on Santa Cruz' portside in 2003.

Home to the Tenerife Symphony Orchestra, the white tsunami design has become an icon of the city and its 1700 seater auditorium witnesses concerts ranging from The Chemical Brothers to The Swirling Dervishes of Cairo.

In the south of the island, diminutive Spanish choreographer Carmen Mota stages shows at the Pirámide de Arona, fusing modern and traditional Spanish dancing in her colourful spectaculars. But the Carmen Mota show is one of the few references to mainland Spain you'll find on Tenerife. For although Madrid may rule their heads, Tinerfeños' hearts belong first to Tenerife and second to Central and South America.

Fiercely protective of their heritage, Tinerfeños of every age know the words to their traditional songs, the steps to their traditional dances and own a '*mago*' or traditional costume. Far from shunning old, outdated ideas, it's predominantly the young who participate in the fiestas which commemorate, celebrate and preserve their heritage, finding any excuse to don the costume and roam the streets amidst traditional bands of '*Parrandas*'. Go along to a teenage party and you're just as likely to hear Los Sabandeños as Muse. In the bars and clubs it's not UK and US chart sounds that dominate, it's Cuban hip hop and salsa, an audible link to Tenerife's Latin American pulse which has been 400 years in the making and which beats its way through the food, the music, the language and of course the Carnaval.

With an over-reliance on mono-cultures throughout its history, every time the island's main cash crop failed due to economic decline, the lure of the New World beckoned and Tinerfeños emigrated in their droves to Cuba, Venezuela and Argentina, founding cities like Montevideo in Uruguay and San Antonio in Texas. With them they took their worship of Nuestra Señora, their wooden carved balconies which became known as 'Colonial' style, the Canarian wrestling of *Lucha Canaria* and the stick fighting of *Juego de Palo*. When they returned, they brought music, food, cigar production and wealth which they invested in building houses and businesses and improving the island's infrastructure.

As a result of this cultural exchange, there's barely a Tenerife family that doesn't have a cousin, a brother or a son who lives in South America and as *Tres Reyes* approaches, queues the length of a football pitch form at the Correos as parcel after parcel waits to be weighed and stamped en route to *Las Américas*.

The unique mix of Tinerfeñan and South American has produced a smiley, friendly people for whom life still moves at a slower pace than for much of the rest of the developed world and for whom time spent with family and friends in their island's benign climate is still far more valuable than money or material possessions.

Long may it remain so.

THE JOYS OF BANKING

"What do you mean you've blocked our account?" My voice rose a few octaves.

The honeymoon period with the bank was clearly over.

In Tenerife, opening a bank account is essential to ensure a continued supply of water, electricity and telephone communication with the outside world as bills are paid direct from your account. The problem is deciding which one to pick. We chose ours because they were a main Spanish bank.

Almost the first communication we received from them was the letter informing us our account had been blocked. We marched to the branch bristling with indignant outrage. The sweet, smiling woman who helped us open our account had been replaced by a hard faced woman with a steely gaze that could crack walnut shells.

"Why is our account blocked?" I asked.

"We ask clients to confirm their tax status every two years," she scowled at me over her glasses. "And you haven't replied."

"But I didn't receive a letter. And anyway, our account is only two months old," I countered.

"No matter," she brushed this point aside. "It's easy to resolve. Sign this," she pushed a document across the desk. "I'll send it to Madrid and within a few days your account will be unblocked."

"Does this mean we won't be able to withdraw any money until then?"

"Oh no, you can withdraw money..." she almost smiled. "...you just can't pay any in."

At that point we realised banking practices here were completely different.

A few months later we were arranging to buy our house and the seller wanted a banker's draft. When we visited the bank to arrange one, they informed us that there would be a charge...of a few hundred euros.

"I'm going to ask them to pass me a phone," I whispered to Andrea.

"Why?" she asked.

"Because I want to phone the police and report that a robbery's in progress and we're the ones being robbed."

Luckily Andrea is far less dramatically inclined and had a flash of inspiration.

"What if we want the money in cash?" she asked the teller. "What charge would there be?"

"None," the teller looked bemused. "There are no charges for withdrawing cash."

And so, three days later we found ourselves in a secure, dark room with two members of staff counting out wads of euros. It saved us a lot of money, but cost the bank hours of staff time. It was only a small victory over bureaucratic madness, but it was incredibly satisfying.

They got their own back though. A year later, we noticed that amidst the charges involved with buying our house, there was one for a couple of hundred euros that we couldn't account for. It was for house insurance which we hadn't asked for nor signed for; the bank had just taken it and as we hadn't queried it at the time, there wasn't a thing we could do about it.

Needless to say we changed our bank.

Jack Montgomery, co-author 'Going Native Tenerife'

FOOD AND DRINK

You might think that after five hundred years of Spanish, Italian, British, Dutch and Portuguese influence, its proximity to Africa and an influx of emigrants returning from South America in the seventies, Tenerife's cuisine would have evolved into a unique fusion of styles. You'd be mistaken. Tinerfeños are incredibly conservative in their culinary tastes and their cuisine, which consists of simply cooked good quality ingredients, reflects this.

Traditional menus have changed little in centuries. Accounts written by travellers in the 18th and 19th centuries describe meals which aren't very different from that which the modern day visitor will be offered.

> *"The staple dish was puchero...which antiquated travellers still call 'olla podrida' (pot pourri)."*
> **Richard Burton, 'To the Gold Coast for Gold'**

On the coast grilled or fried fish is the norm and what a choice; sea bass, snapper, sole, hake, monkfish, swordfish and even shark. However, if you're going to eat only one fish on Tenerife it should be *vieja* (parrot fish); its sublime smoky flavours have earned it the distinction of being the islanders' favourite fish. Another popular and wallet friendly choice is *cherne* (grouper); a meaty fish similar to cod and ideal for anyone who gets bored picking bones out of their teeth.

Inland is more traditional country fare; huge slabs of meat cooked on wood burning grills, *conejo en salmorejo* (rabbit in sauce) and hearty stews like Burton's *puchero* (an 'everything but the kitchen sink' mix which usually includes chickpeas, pumpkin, potatoes, carrots, beans, corn and whatever leftover meat is to hand) warm the cockles against the sometimes brisk mountain air.

Meals are usually served with '*papas arrugadas*' (delicious small potatoes boiled in seriously salty water until they wrinkle) and two sauces - *mojo verde* and *mojo rojo*; one made from coriander, the other from chillies (one of the few spicy items found on menus).

An ingredient which predates the Spanish conquest is *gofio* (toasted cereals) which was a staple of the islands' original inhabitants, the Guanche. It's still used extensively today to thicken and flavour stews, or is mixed with cheese or nuts and cut it into small cakes (*asado*). Gofio is also a kind of forerunner to power drinks; Jesús, a gofio mill worker in La Orotava, swears by it saying that a glass of gofio and milk in the morning gives him energy and staves off hunger until lunchtime.

Most people probably wouldn't think of the Canary Islands as wine growing country, yet Shakespeare received a barrel of Canarian Malmsey wine as part of his annual salary and often sang its praises in his plays. The island has over 100 vineyards which produce some fine wines which are good enough to have you...well, if not singing their praises, at least singing. The island's diverse microclimates mean that although the grapes grown are similar, mainly Listans and Negramolls, flavours vary from one area to the next. Wines which consistently earn the most accolades are the Viña Norte range from the Bodegas Insulares in Tacoronte; personally I think the wines from Bodega El Lomo in Tegueste, which are as smooth as James Bond in a tux, are just as good, but then I'm equally happy quaffing some 'vino del país' (good, honest country wine usually from the owner's small plot) in a local tasca.

TRANSPORT

With two international airports, flying to Tenerife from just about anywhere in Europe is relatively easy and not overly expensive. There are flights from most main British airports to **Reina Sofia** airport in the south of the island, located only a short distance from the main resorts. **Los Rodeos**, near La Laguna, is better placed for accessing the north and Santa Cruz and receives more traffic from mainland Spain as well as inter-island flights; Binter Airways (*www.bintercanarias.com*) fly daily to all the other Canary Islands.

The TF1 autopista (Tenerife's version of a motorway) connects the south with Santa Cruz, linking with the TF5 at Santa Maria del Mar, the northern autopista then stretches to Los Realejos. In theory, it's the quickest way to get from the north to the south of the island; the journey from Puerto de la Cruz to Playa de Las Américas taking roughly an hour and a half. Attempt it on a Monday morning and you can double that time.

The motorway between Santa Cruz and La Laguna is congested during morning rush hour (which seems to last until about 11.00am) and can test the nerves of the most confident driver. In 2007, the tranvia (*www.tranviatenerife.com*) was introduced, linking the two cities and reducing some of the traffic on the road. These colourful trams are a cheap (€1.25 single journey) and stress free way to commute between the capital and La Laguna. Plans to add a second line are underway and a light railway connecting Santa Cruz with the south is also in the pipeline.

Although the autopistas are a practical way of getting from A to B quickly, country roads are a much more interesting and enjoyable way of getting around the island. Most roads are in decent condition with much less traffic. The main drawback for nervous drivers is that some roads twist and turn over precipitous drops. It adds a little spice to journeys, but it's worth it; views are spectacular. With over one hundred car rental firms on Tenerife, hiring a car isn't a problem; most are reliable and the longer the rental, the better the deal.

For non-drivers, Tenerife has an excellent public bus service, Titsa (*www.titsa.com*). Known as Gua-Guas (pronounced Wah-Wahs; locals say because of the noise made by their horns when they were first introduced) buses are clean, comfortable and relatively punctual. Routes cover every town and village on the island; although the more rural the location, the more limited the service is likely to be. The best bases for exploring Tenerife by bus are Santa Cruz, La Laguna, Puerto de la Cruz and to a lesser extent, Playa de Las Américas and Los Cristianos. A Bono ticket (€12 & €30; available from bus stations and some shops) reduces fares by up to 50%.

Tram - Santa Cruz de Tenerife

It's still possible to arrive in Tenerife the old fashioned way, by boat. Trasmediterranea (*www.trasmediterranea.es*) operates a crossing from Cadiz which takes two days. Naviera Armas (*www.navieraarmas.com*), Fred Olsen (*www.fredolsen.es*) and the Garajonay Exprés (*www.garajonayexpres.com*) also run ferries to other Canary Islands departing from Santa Cruz and Los Cristianos.

THE GREEN MILES - A NON-DRIVER'S HOMAGE TO TENERIFE'S BUSES

Pumping out hot engine fumes, and dribbling air conditioning fluid, the engine ticks over as the driver goes for a coffee. Green merely describes the colour of the single decker TITSA (*www.titsa.com*) public service buses that I have grown to love during 7 years in Tenerife.

They rattle, swinging round the tight corners as they criss cross Tenerife, and it seems more than just religious fervour as old Canarian women make the sign of the cross at every new sheer drop we pass. Despite this, I am a big fan, and armed with my 12 or 30 euro Bono discount ticket, I often take off for a little adventure around the island.

The Bono gives about a third off any journey plus a convoluted series of further sliding discounts when you change to another of their buses, but from Los Cristianos in the south to Santa Cruz in the north is a mere 4.45 euros one way. The Bono is also good for the Santa Cruz tram and will reap entry discounts at any of the 4 major museums in the north.

I always allow plenty of room for no shows and late buses, but most of the time, the buses are pretty reliable, try running this past your local union – they run every day of the year including Christmas and all their own fiesta days. Some rural bus stops are little more than a big stone with a post by it, yet people will jump off and reclaim their dozen or so carrier bags of shopping from the roomy boot underneath and stroll off seemingly in the middle of rolling fields bordered by large mountains.

Buses are big, bigger than cars, therefore they can take more liberties and parp their horns louder than car drivers, well that seems to be their theory. I'm not arguing, I have great respect for the drivers, not only do they have to wear an awful grey and green striped shirt (the cardigan really is the final insult but thankfully rarely needed), they also have to negotiate tight bends, hire car drivers from hell and tourists that have large cash point notes, no idea of where they are going and an all consuming hurry to get there quickly.

Most routes don't run much past midnight, but they put on extra buses for Carnaval and other big events, then they are packed with people in fancy dress, clanking bags full of bottles and loads of dancing. Another good game is to compare and contrast, the lively late bus at night into the nightclub south, and the first few home in the morning, full of sleepy zombies.

But I will hear nothing but praise for these buses, grab your Bono, board your TITSA and pick a random destination, it's great fun.

Colin Kirby, freelance writer, *www.colinkirby.com*

CLIMATE

Generally weather forecasts for Tenerife are a bit like 'The Curate's Egg'; they're never completely accurate, but neither are they completely inaccurate.

The problem derives from the fact that Tenerife is made up of a series of diverse microclimates. When there are clear blue skies in one area, it can look as though the end of the world is about to arrive a few kilometres further along the coast. The one thing that's certain is that it's very rare for the sun not to be shining somewhere on Tenerife.

As a rule though, there are general patterns that visitors can expect to find in different geographical locations across Tenerife.

South and south west coasts tend to experience the most sunshine and the least rain and subsequently are the warmest parts of the island. The price of this is that they are also dry and barren; good for sun seeking tourists, but not for farmers.

The east coast also benefits from hot, sunny weather but, like many east coasts, can be breezy; the fact that the wind farms are on the south east coast are a bit of a giveaway.

Trade winds from the north east bring seas of clouds and rain to northern slopes during parts of the year. These clouds settle into folds in the hills between the 600 to 1800 metre mark; spectacular if you happen to be above them, but can be dreary if caught underneath, or even worse actually in them. Their influence means that temperatures on the northern coasts are a few degrees lower than their southern counterparts and there's more of a likelihood of rain (except during June – August when there's virtually no rainfall on any coast). The upside is that the northern countryside is lush and sub-tropical.

As soon as you move inland, and therefore uphill, temperatures drop. It's not so noticeable during summer months, but for the rest of the year it can get positively nippy. In the winter temperatures on Mount Teide's summit can plummet to -10 when the sun drops.

Between November and April, winter snows regularly cloak Mount Teide in a white overcoat, making the mountain even more impressive than usual, especially when viewed from the warmth of the beach. Snow levels can reach the 2000 metre mark and it's not uncommon for roads to the crater to be closed during the heaviest of the snowfalls.

A common weather phenomenon which affects mainly the southern coast is *'calima'*, a hot dusty wind which blows in from the Sahara. For approximately three days, temperatures soar to unbearable levels and the hot, dry wind turns the air amber, leaving everything covered in a thin layer of sand.

One thing that is constant is the temperature of the sea; it's pretty much the same on all coasts and varies only a few degrees between winter and summer (19 to 23 degrees), so is always pleasant for swimming.

Temperature

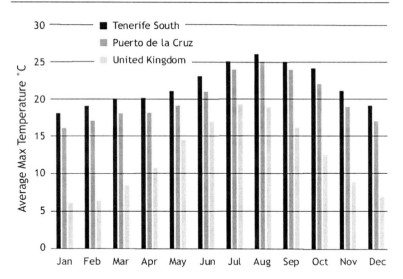

Rainfall

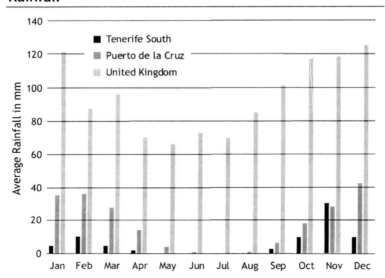

Sunshine

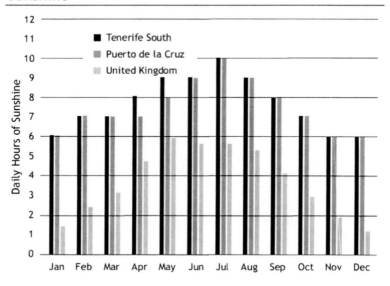

ECONOMY

Unemployment in Tenerife (16% June 2008) is higher than the national average for Spain (10% June 2008), but that doesn't necessarily paint an accurate picture of job prospects.

With tourism being the main industry (accounting for more than 60% of its GDP), the job market is very much a transient one and, in the southern resorts especially, there are many 'casual' jobs which don't make it onto the official radar and subsequently are never included in employment statistics.

Again because the market is such a transient one with people taking bar work to finance extended holidays, there are always jobs available for waiters, bar staff, sales, PR personnel and gardeners. Anyone that can hold a tune and play an instrument should also find work relatively easily as there are always places looking for entertainers.

The paradox however, is that most of these are located in the purpose built tourist resorts in the south of the island, so anyone seeking to experience the true culture of Tenerife, and therefore basing themselves outside of the main resorts, may encounter more difficulties in finding employment.

Whilst establishments in the north of the island also regularly display '*se falta camarero/a*' notices; being able to speak Spanish is generally a prerequisite.

The Tenerife Forum website (*www.tenerifeforum.com*) is a good source of what opportunities are available and includes links to both English and Spanish job pages. If possible, it's worth checking whether prospective employers are reliable payers; a lackadaisical approach to coughing up wages is not uncommon. A hassle free way to sort out accommodation and employment prior to arrival is to use an agency like Playaway (*www.playawaytenerife.com*).

The housing market is also disparate in relation to prices in the north and south of the island. Property can cost up to 30% more in southern areas, especially those considered fashionable. For the price of a two bedroom apartment in Adeje you could have a three, or even four bedroomed one in Los Realejos. The same formula can be applied to long term rentals.

Estate agents attribute this to the guarantee of more sunshine on the south coast, the Holy Grail for many; although cynics would say that these areas also invariably attract expatriates who are willing to pay more than Canarios.

Prices decrease with the temperature; the further inland you go, and therefore uphill, the more you get for your money and there are still some very good bargains to be had on Tenerife's hillsides.

Businesses come and go overnight in Tenerife, sometimes taking clients' hard earned money with them, so choosing the right *inmobiliaria* (estate agent) is essential. The safest bet is to opt for one which has been established for some time. It's common practice for the same property to be advertised in various *inmobiliarias*, often with different asking prices. Even then, advertised prices are little more than guidelines. Tell an estate agent that you like a property, but the price is way too high and in response they might pick up a piece of scrap paper, unconvincingly scribble some figures on it and then knock twenty thousand euros off the asking price. It's always worthwhile trying to haggle.

FIESTA CALENDAR

January 5th: Epiphany, Island wide

The children's fiesta; on the night before the Epiphany, the *Tres Reyes* (Three Kings) arrive in towns all over the island (on camels in La Orotava, Garachico and Los Cristianos) bestowing gifts and throwing sweets to the crowds with such enthusiasm it could have your eye out.

January 17th: San Abad, Buenavista del Norte

Over 1500 oxen, goats, horses, donkeys and...guinea pigs put in an appearance.

February/March (exact dates affected by Easter): Carnaval, Santa Cruz and Puerto de la Cruz

The biggest fiesta of the year and the time to slip on the fishnets and sexy little black number, if your wife will let you, and join the week long party.

April: Semana Santa (Easter), La Laguna and Adeje

The serious fiesta; solemn, silent and evocative processions involving cloaked brotherhoods on Viernes Santo (Good Friday).

The Passion of Christ - Most of the townspeople take on roles in an enthusiastic and biblical sized re-enactment of the crucifixion in Adeje on Good Friday.

April 25th (Sunday closest to): San Marcos, Icod de los Vinos and Tegueste

Galleons on wheels lead Tegueste's colourful and bizarre Romería.

May 3rd: Fiestas of the Cross, Santa Cruz, Puerto de la Cruz and Los Realejos

Crosses are ornately decorated on the streets and in houses, but let's be honest, it's the three hour long firework display in Los Realejos we really want to see.

June (exact dates affected by Easter): Corpus Christi, La Orotava, Santa Cruz, La Laguna and Tacoronte

Flower power in La Orotava when the old cobbled streets are carpeted with beautifully ornate floral images...only to be trampled on by the clergy. Carpets are also created in Santa Cruz, La Laguna and Tacoronte.

June (Sunday following Corpus Christi): Romería, La Ortova

One of the largest on the island with beauty queens on camels, over 70 carts pulled by oxen, traditional singers and dancers and as much wine and food as you can catch.

June 23rd & 24th: San Juan, Puerto de la Cruz

On the night of the 23rd there's a huge party on Playa Jardín – bring your own candles, flowers and food and be prepared for a midnight dip. The following morning the town's harbour is filled with goats in honour of an ancient Guanche ritual.

July 16th (week including): Virgin del Carmen, fishing communities all over Tenerife, particularly Puerto de la Cruz

Mariners carry their patron saint through the streets before taking her on a sea trip (Santa Cruz, Puerto de la Cruz, Las Galletas). Alcalá swims against the tide, holding theirs on 15th August.

July 25th: Anniversary of Nelson's defeat, Santa Cruz

The capital celebrates the defeat of Nelson in 1797 by staging a re-enactment of the heroic defence of the city. Brits can participate as long as they don't mind losing.

August 14th & 15th: Nuestra Señora de Candelaria, Candelaria

Pilgrims travel (many on foot) from all over the island to celebrate their Patron Saint's day...and watch a couple of cavemen do a Laurel & Hardy routine.

August 16th: San Roque, Garachico

Free food and drink dished out by lads and lassies in colourful traditional costumes on oxen drawn carts.

August 18th: Fiestas del Santísimo Cristo, La Laguna

One of Tenerife's most beloved icons, a Gothic carving of the crucifixion, is paraded through the town.

August 24th: Hearts of Tejina, Tejina

The townsfolk of La Tejina construct giant hearts from flowers and fruit and hurl insults at each other.

September 7th: Fiestas Del Socorro, Güímar

The people of Güímar carry their Patron Saint's image across the malpaís to a sanctuary by the sea.

October 12th: Día de la Hispanidad, Island wide

Anniversary of Columbus' discovery of the New World and a public holiday.

November 29th: San Andrés, Puerto de la Cruz and Icod de los Vinos

An excuse for quaffing the new wines in Puerto de La Cruz and then careening down an almost vertical hill on a metal tray in Icod de los Vinos.

December (first week): Fiesta del Cuento, Los Silos

Los Silos becomes even more enchanting during the International Storytelling Festival.

GOING NATIVE IN TENERIFE
Families

Weekend

Buy a twin ticket and try to pack in the dolphin, orca, sea lion and parrot shows in one day at Loro Parque in Puerto de la Cruz. Next day get into the swimwear and find out which family members are brave enough to launch themselves from a tower and through a pool of piranhas and alligators at Siam Park in Costa Adeje.

Week

Get up close and personal with some cheeky monkeys at the Monkey Park near Los Cristianos.

Find your sea legs and meet some of the dolphins and whales which cavort in the straits between Tenerife and La Gomera on a boat trip from Los Gigantes or Puerto Colón.

If you haven't seen enough animal parks by now, the Las Aguilas Jungle Park at Chayofa should keep the David Attenborough's amongst the family happy.

Month

Test everybody's vertigo with the cable car trip which ascends to five hundred metres below the summit of Mount Teide. The views are stupendous and the sulphurous smells will have the kids sniggering 'who dealt it?'

To avoid the snack bars in the crater relieving you of your dosh faster than a pick pocket, pack a picnic and eat al fresco in the recreation zone at Las Lajas.

Save on the petrol and see most of Tenerife in a couple of hours. The model village of PuebloChico in La Orotava has beautifully detailed layouts of the best of the island and is full of humorous touches.

You haven't really experienced Tenerife until you can say that you've swum in Garachico's rock pools. Shallow pools with tropical fish, deep plunge pools and narrow channels in the volcanic rock create a natural water park that everyone can enjoy.

Saddle up that camel and ride off into the...err forest. If you can put up with the tacky mock Arab garb, it's a good way to see the lush scenery around the Camel Park at El Tanque. The arid countryside around the other Camel Park at La Camella is a more authentic, if a less attractive setting.

You've got to teach the kids the song before you take them on a voyage beneath the waves in the, yep you've got it...Yellow Submarine, from San Miguel Marina.

If the unthinkable happens and it rains, go to the Museum of Science and Cosmos in La Laguna to chase away the grey skies. Many of the interactive exhibits are designed to make mum and dad look very silly; laughter in a museum...whatever next?

For Life

Kids will love the Three Kings parade with its fancy floats and free sweets galore on the 5th of January (the Spanish version of Christmas Eve), especially in the towns where the kings arrive on camels (Garachico, La Orotava, Los Cristianos).

Overdose on one of the most spectacular firework displays you're likely to see anywhere at the three hour extravagance in Los Realejos during the Fiestas of the Cross in May.

Culture Vultures

Weekend

Stroll La Orotava's atmospheric old streets visiting the Casas de Los Balcones and the Iberoamerican museum, ensuring you end up at Casa Lercaro for a tapas lunch overlooking the prettiest courtyard of them all.

Dress up to the nines for a night at the opera, ballet, or jazz concert in Santa Cruz' iconic and stunning Auditorio de Tenerife; it's proof that modern architecture can be beautiful.

Follow the sculpture trail along Las Ramblas in Santa Cruz, discovering wonderful pieces by Henry Moore and Joan Miró along the way and stopping for the occasional café cortado at one of the pavement cafés.

Week

Spend a couple of hours exploring the Canary Island's unluckiest town, picturesque Garachico and enjoy a glass of wine at the kiosk overlooking the prettiest plaza on Tenerife.

Step back in time on La Laguna's perfectly preserved streets, a UNESCO World Heritage Site, ducking into a darkened doorway of a tasca for refreshments when energy levels drop.

Feel the passion of Flamenco at the Carmen Mota Ballet in Playa de Las Américas.

Month

Are they real, or are they a hoax? The Pyramids of Güímar are the source of heated debates. Visit these mysterious constructions set in tranquil grounds and decide for yourself.

Get under the skin of Tenerife's natural history at the Museum of Man and Nature in Santa Cruz; one of the only places you can see original Guanche inhabitants of Tenerife in the flesh.

It's not necessary to wait until August to make a pilgrimage to Candelaria to view the patron saint of the Canary Islands and the nine original kings of Tenerife who stand proudly in front of the impressive basilica.

If you don't have time to visit the hundred plus bodegas on Tenerife, the wine museum and restaurant in El Sauzal is as good as place as any to find out why the island's Malmsey wine made Shakespeare wax lyrical.

Learn how the lords and ladies of Tenerife's manors used to live at Tenerife's 'secret' Anthropological Museum in Valle de Guerra.

If you want to discover exactly how Lord Nelson lost his right arm, the excellent Military Museum in Santa Cruz can set you right...in great detail.

For Life

Witness one of the most evocative processions you're ever likely to see during La Laguna's 'Magna' and 'Silent Processions' at Semana Santa.

Fawn over La Orotava's flower carpets during Corpus Christi and when the feet get tired, abscond to a 'Guachinche' (makeshift bar) for pinchos and wine.

Get right in amongst the goats and boats at 'El baño de las cabras' in the harbour at Puerto de la Cruz on Midsummer's day.

Cry with everybody else when the singer strikes up 'Ave Maria' and the Virgen del Carmen is carefully loaded on a boat during the fiestas in fishing communities in July.

Eat, drink and definitely be merry, all for free, at any one of Tenerife's harvest romerías which take place in towns all over the island between May and October.

Don't take it personally if you're insulted at the unique Hearts of Tejina fiesta in the town of the same name near La Laguna. It's part and parcel of the tradition which involves the raising of three giant fruit, cereal and vegetable hearts outside of the church.

Plonk yourself down at a table overlooking the harbour in Puerto de la Cruz on the eve of San Andrés and order a beaker of country wine and a poke of roasted chestnuts to celebrate the arrival of the season's new wines.

GUEST OF HONOUR

A few weeks after touching down on the island, we found ourselves, courtesy of a friend's boss, sharing a table with the guests of honour, the Irish Consul to Tenerife and his wife, at Tenerife's annual Wine Awards. The couple arrived late, just as the lights had been dimmed and the awards were about to begin.

Andrea was wearing her favourite cocktail dress and I, my kilt. It transpired that the Consul had Scottish ancestors so we chatted away about Scotland until it was time for the winners to be announced at which time the Canarian presenter gestured towards our table and thanked the Consul for attending.

As soon as the awards were over, the band struck up and the Consul and his wife headed to the dance floor whilst Andrea and I concentrated on testing more of the wines on the table. I was enjoying a full bodied red when I heard an English voice in my ear.

"Do you mind if I take you and your wife's photograph?" I didn't know him then, but it was Joe Cawley, author of 'More Ketchup than Salsa' and editor of Living Tenerife Magazine at the time.

"Sure," Andrea and I smiled for the camera and Joe clicked away.

"Thanks," Joe stood up. "Oh, what's your wife's name?"

"Andrea," I answered.

As he moved away, a thought occurred to me. Why hadn't he asked for my name?

When the Consul returned to the table he said that it was time for him and his wife to leave. He bade his goodbyes and made his way to the exit, stopping and chatting to someone he knew on the way.

A few moments later the presenter of the awards came over and shook my hand.

"Thank you for coming tonight," he gushed. "I hope you've enjoyed yourselves?"

"It's been absolutely lovely," Andrea replied.

He smiled and walked away; however, I noticed that he hadn't thanked anyone else at the table.

"Something's wrong," I whispered to Andrea. "I'm pretty sure they think I'm the Irish Consul and they've completely ignored the real Consul."

I felt a cold sweat break out on my forehead. I could see the headlines:

"British couple deported from Tenerife for impersonating the Irish Consul and his wife."

I had to do something, and quickly; the Consul was nearly at the exit. I saw Joe heading into the gents and followed him.

"Hi, again, who do you think I am?" I asked.

"You're the Irish Consul," Joe answered.

"Wrong," I pointed at the door. "He's out there and just about to leave."

"Oh, right, cheers," Joe grabbed his camera and made a hasty exit.

Next, I sought out the presenter.

"There's been a bit of a mix up. Who do you think I am?"

"You're the Irish," his eyes dropped to my kilt. "...Oh my god, you're Scottish." He slapped his forehead; all that was missing was a "DOH".

I pointed him in the direction of the Consul, returned to our table, sat down and took a great slug of wine relieved that, having barely set foot on the island, I hadn't inadvertently been the cause of an embarrassing international incident.

Jack Montgomery, co-author 'Going Native Tenerife'

Nature Lovers

Weekend

Descend into a prehistoric world by trekking deep into the Masca Barranco. Take a bocadillo to munch on at Masca bay while you wait for the catamaran to come and transport you back to the present.

Lose yourself in a maze of unusual tropical vegetation at the Botanical Gardens in Puerto de la Cruz and become at one with nature at the serene lily pond.

Gaze upon one of the oldest living things on the planet, the mythical multi-headed Millenium Drago Tree in Icod de los Vinos before immersing yourself in a world of colour at the 'El Mariposeria' butterfly farm.

Week

Explore remotest Tenerife's Laurasilva forests and valleys by following the trail from Cruz del Carmen in the Anaga Mountains to the troglodyte community at Chinamada where you can enjoy lunch in a cave.

Moon walk without the need for a spacesuit; leave the crowds in the Las Cañadas del Teide crater and strike out into a landscape which truly deserves its other worldly tag.

Enter Hell's ravine (Barranco del Infierno) if you dare, to find a rare sight on Tenerife, a waterfall. Afterwards, unlace the hiking boots and tuck into the local speciality, garlic chicken at one of the nearby restaurants.

Month

Head deep into the pines and across the La Orotava valley starting and finishing at the log bar in La Caldera where you can down a cerveza in the company of chaffinches, blue jays and robins.

Join a select club and seek out the mysterious and surreal 'Paisajes Lunar' in the hills above Vilaflor, refilling water flasks with sweet spring water at the Madre del Agua campsite before returning to Vilaflor and relaxing on the terrace of the La Paz café.

Coast along the old merchants' trail at Las Ramblas del Castro, passing palm groves, animal shaped rocks and a fort overlooking secret coves, before finishing at the San Telmo mirador for a sundowner and views of Tenerife's most stunning coastline.

For Life

Buy a tent and try camping the old fashioned way. Pitch the canvas in one of the dedicated camping zones in the heart of the forests all around the island and the chances are it'll just be you and the trees under a cloak of sparkling stars.

Sport Enthusiasts

Weekend

Squeeze into the wetsuit, grab the board and make friends with the wind at Tenerife's colourful windsurfing and kite-boarding capital, El Médano. Then chill out with the rest of the surf dudes at Flashpoint.

Discover more of Tenerife's diverse scenery, this time under the waves. You don't need to be Jacques Cousteau to mix it with schools of rays, tuna and barracuda which add life to rusting shipwrecks, caves and basaltic rock formations near Las Galletas.

Week

Believe you can fly; paraglide from Izaña, Adeje, or Los Realejos for a bird's eye view of the island. If the idea of going solo brings on the sweats, you can always try tandem.

Surf dream waves at El Socorro beach on the north west coast where winter crests can reach eight metres. If you don't want a wipe out, order a plate of *camerones* and watch the professionals from the beach bar.

Tee up at Tenerife's most dramatic golf course in Buenavista del Norte. Its distance from the main tourist drags makes it feel like your own private course. After a taxing round, or two, cool off in the exquisite infinity pool set into the rocks beside the course.

Month

Grow a beard (optional) à la Hemmingway and head out to sea in search of marlin, tuna and any other big fish that inhabit the waters around Los Cristianos harbour.

Get really high by climbing Mount Teide and spending a night in the Altavista refuge before reaching the summit in time for sunrise to witness the phenomena known as 'Teide's shadow'.

Go all Spiderman by trying to negotiate seemingly impossible overhangs and sheer rock walls in the rock climber's natural adventure park around Arico.

For Life

Paint your face blue and white, buy a giant Tweety Pie and beat the stuffing out of it when the Las Palmas player's coach arrives for the football derby between Los Blanquiazuls, (CD Tenerife) and Los Canarios, (arch rivals, Las Palmas from Gran Canaria) in Santa Cruz. It's a family affair really, all good fun and a great way to integrate.

INTO THE CRATER

The request was as surprising as it was unique. 'I want a walk that hurts', said Ieuan (pronounced eye-an). I was guiding the energetic Welshman and his friend Steve on a walk to the summit of a prominent mountain, close to my home in south Tenerife, when he made his unusual request. The day had been something of a compromise as Steve was not a committed walker and the climb represented an easy half-day out for Ieuan. He now wanted to be tested on something much harder. 'I want a minimum of 3,000ft of ascent, something to really stretch the legs', he said. 'I'll see what I can come up with', I said, slightly worried. I had a days rest to let my legs recover and to come up with a route to satisfy Ieuan's masochistic request.

Unlike Ieuan, most walkers prefer to limit the amount of hills in a walk, so the routes I normally use are within the average walkers comfort zone. Certainly, none of them involved 3,000ft of ascent. I racked my brains before realising I had a route that involved 3,300ft of *descent*. What about doing it in reverse! The route, from the parador in the Las Cañadas National Park to Vilaflor, Spain's highest village, normally involves a climb of around 1,000ft from the huge caldera before descending to Vilaflor. By reversing the route, I would have an ascent of around 3,300ft and a descent of 1,000ft to the parador. Perfect!

On the day of the walk we set-off from the statue of Hermano Pedro in the square in Vilaflor and were soon climbing steeply beneath a cloudless sky, following the newly restored path to the Lunar Landscape. This impressive path, winding its way through pines and across steep barrancos, eliminated the need to walk along the tedious Pista del Madre Agua dirt-road. After just under two hours of uphill walking, we left the path and began climbing more steeply towards the caldera rim.

As we ascended through the wild beauty of the Barranco de Eris towards the caldera rim far above, the walking became much harder and looking back, I saw Ieuan was feeling it too. It seemed that the altitude was beginning to have an effect and we stopped frequently for breath and to enjoy the views of the surrounding mountains. Continuing, we came below the rugged, overhanging cliffs of Montana Guajara, which signalled that we were closing in on our goal when the summit of Teide suddenly rose majestically into view above the caldera rim. We were on the summit of the pass. Ieuan let out a whoop of elation and warmly shook my hand. 'That's what I call a walk', he said.

Below, the miniature tourist buses gleamed in the sun as holidaymakers climbed over the Roques de Garcia. Distracting Ieuan's gaze from the summit of Guajara with the lure of a beer at the parador, we began to descend. After 3.5 hours of mostly steep, uphill climbing, the descent was a pleasure. It had definitely been 'a walk that hurt', and I had a sense of accomplishment but at the same time relief, that I could now relax and enjoy the stunning scenery of my beautiful island home as we descended for that much anticipated and hard-earned beer.

Gary Rosson, Guided Walks, *www.cyberhiker.co.uk*

Hopeless Romantics

Weekend

Buy a bottle of cava, then stock up on sensual sweets from the chocolate cave at El Aderno in Los Silos. Drive to the Punto Teno lighthouse and toast the sun as it sets behind La Gomera before retiring to the enchanting setting of the San Roque Hotel in Garachico.

Indulge in a decadent Champagne breakfast at the Mirador Café in the grounds of El Monasterio, overlooking the La Orotava Valley. Head into Santa Cruz and take a stroll in poets and lover's favourite, Parque García Sanabria. Drive along the spine of the island to spend a night at the Parador in the centre of Las Cañadas del Teide. Warm up with a brandy beside the hotel's log fire and cuddle up under the gaze of some of the clearest night skies on the planet.

Party Animals

Weekend

Compare and contrast the clubbing scene north and south. Head to the holiday maker's nightclub centre around Veronicas in Playa de Las Américas and the choice of dance, trance and R & B at top tourist favourites, Tramps, Rags and Bobby's, or join the smart set at Liquid, the Canarian's choice.

Next night hit the bright lights of Avenida Generalisimo in Puerto de la Cruz where almost fifteen clubs meet the dancing demands of the clubbers of north Tenerife. Being a Canarian scene, some hip-hop salsa lessons might be needed.

For Life

In February/March, dress as outrageously as you dare and salsa every night for a week with thousands of other weird and wonderfully decked out revellers at the biggest street parties in the world outside Rio during 'Carnaval' in Santa Cruz and Puerto de la Cruz.

Get the blues at the Santa Cruz blues festival in June. Join the 'in crowd' in the Noria district and listen to some of the biggest names in blues music until midnight, then hit the seriously stylish bars on the capital's coolest street.

Dig a hole, fill it with flowers and candles, uncork a bottle of vino and lie back in the sand to listen to the music on Playa Jardín in Puerto de la Cruz at the Fiesta de San Juan in June. At midnight, strip off and head to the sea with everybody else to bathe in the magical midsummer waters.

If you've got the stamina, listen through 30 hours of live music at the Aguaviva festival at the end of June in Los Cristianos.

Support the environment and get to listen to some great Spanish and International bands at the two day Eolica festival at Granadilla's Renewable Energy Institute in July.

Techno, house, garage, grunge hip-hop – you'd better gen up on your familiarity with dance music speak to get the best of the sounds that up to forty DJs blast out during the dusk till dawn Inspirations fiesta in Puerto de la Cruz in summer.

Town and City Guide

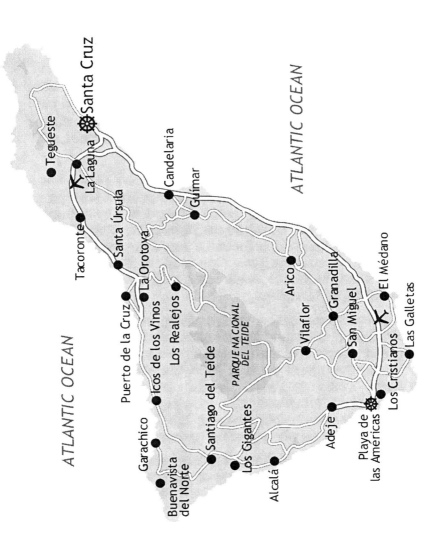

NORTH TENERIFE

"...Under the torrid zone I found sites where nature is more majestic and richer in the display of organic forms; but after having traversed the banks of the Orinoco, the Cordilleras of Peru, and the most beautiful valleys of Mexico, I own that I have never beheld a prospect more varied, more attractive, more harmonious in the distribution of the masses of verdure and rocks, than the western coast of Teneriffe."
Alexander von Humboldt, June 1799

When he uttered these words, Von Humboldt was gazing from Tacoronte across the La Orotava Valley and what today is referred to as the northern coast. And although two centuries of development would probably prevent him from considering the view today as the best he had ever seen, he would surely agree that it is still the most beautiful in Tenerife.

A few degrees cooler and receiving more rainfall than the rest of the island in a climate referred to as 'eternal spring', from the most westerly town of Buenavista to the north-eastern point of Punta de Hidalgo, Tenerife's north coast is lush, fertile and green. Banana plantations, vines and palm groves carpet the cultivated landscape which falls down to the Atlantic, carved by deep barrancos where the indigenous flora thrives.

From the north, without a crater wall to mask it, the true magnitude and beauty of Mount Teide dominates the horizon, acting as a constant reminder that you're at the foot of Europe's largest volcano and Spain's highest mountain.

Puerto de la Cruz is the area's main tourist resort while in the valley above it lies the Colonial town of La Orotava, generally agreed to be the most picturesque of all Tenerife's towns. Further to the west are the historic port of Garachico with its volcanic rock pools and the busy town of Icod de los Vinos, home to the famous Millennium Drago Tree.

> *"If there's water in Puerto, there's no electricity…*
> *if there's electricity, there's no water."*
> **José – gardener, slightly exaggerating**
> **Puerto de la Cruz' temperamental utilities**

The former capital city of La Laguna forms part of a necklace of towns, strung above the north motorway; hidden gems that many of the millions of visitors to Tenerife never see.

A thousand miles away from the busy beaches of the south, this is where you'll find the true Tenerife; its food, culture, history and people; where English is not widely spoken and you have only to step outside of your door to know that you are in a foreign country.

Bajamar/Punta de Hidalgo

Almost on the northernmost tip, the twin towns of Bajamar and Punta de Hidalgo are Tenerife's forgotten resorts.

Their setting, a stunning Anaga Mountain backdrop, makes the sight of the unattractive concrete apartment blocks which greet visitors on arrival all the more depressing.

Originally a small agricultural farming and fishing community, the area was developed in the 1930s as a summer retreat for residents from La Laguna. When mass tourism took off in the late 1960s, a clutch of hotels and apartments were constructed; however, the opening of the south airport put a kybosh on its chances of making a real impact on the tourist market and the area fell into decline. First impressions are that both Bajamar and Punta de Hidalgo are still in decline; they resemble tired 70s resorts and the peeling plaster on some buildings doesn't help with the run down image.

Recently there have been promising changes; the promenades in both have been given a makeover and the development of the seafront in Bajamar to incorporate smart wooden decking and tubular aluminium seating around the sea water pools has given the resort a contemporary kick up the backside. In Punta de Hidalgo a wide, palmtree lined walkway leads to a tiny sheltered harbour which feels more Cornish than Canarian; a reminder of the charming spot that this must have been before unimaginative architects left their mark on the landscape.

Between July and September, the area is a summer favourite for Lagueros; the rest of the year it's popular with mainly German visitors who use it as a base to explore the Anaga Mountains.

Beaches

The coastline's rocky, that's not to say there aren't plenty of places for swimming. Man made pools in Punta de Hidalgo, Bajamar and Charco de la Arena beyond the lighthouse blend nicely into the basaltic rock and offer protection from the Atlantic rollers. There's a small imported golden sand beach in Bajamar's sheltered harbour; although most people prefer the wooden decking for sunbathing. A rocky beach links the two resorts, but unless you're accomplished on a surfboard (competitions are held here), it's probably better to stick to the safety of the pools.

Food

Cofradias de Pescadores (Fishermen's Guilds) are always a safe bet for good local fish dishes and Punta de

Hidalgo's (922 15 69 54; Avda Marítimo, 56;) overlooking the harbour, is no exception. *Morena Frita* (fried moray eel) is a local speciality. It has a delicate flavour, but the bones can be tiresome. Anyone who doesn't like to know their food had a life prior to arriving on their plate should steer clear of the tables closest to the harbour; they're only a few feet from where fishermen gut the eels.

Accommodation

Apart from the **Océano Aparthotel** in Punta de Hidalgo (922 15 60 00; C/Océanico Pacifico, 1; *www.oceano.de*), which is also a spa centre, hotels are dated and not very appealing.

Attractions

At early morning, follow the coastal path beyond Punta de Hidalgo's lighthouse to the viewpoint at the small ermita of San Juanita. The vista, as the sun bathes the rugged Tolkienesque coastline with shafts of light, is mythical.

Buenavista del Norte

"There's the library," pointed the man from outside the bar as I got out of my car in Buenavista, *"and around the corner's the church. That's it, you've seen all there is to see!"*

He was kidding of course...just.

Capital of the Isla Baja region that hugs the north west corner of Tenerife, Buenavista feels like the place you pass through en route to the golf course or the lighthouse, the place where there seems to be constant construction work, despite the fact that it looks devoid of people or life.

In reality, it has a very nice old quarter around Plaza de Nuestra Señora de Los Remedios tucked away behind the main road and is in fact one of the oldest settlements on Tenerife.

But its more modern face is bereft of character and sprawls its way beyond the old plaza to the coast and ever further westwards towards Punta de Teno.

Beaches

Head towards the golf course to get to Playa de las Arenas; a black sand and pebble beach adorned by rock pools and extremely popular in summer. The beach has no facilities save for a kiosk selling ice creams and sweets, but there's a wonderful, scenic coastal path that runs from the golf course to the westerly headland with lots of side paths leading to viewing platforms and hidden rock pools.

Food

Restaurants are another of Buenavista's Achilles' Heels. In the town itself, they're conspicuous by their absence but at the beach, **El Burgado** (922 12 78 31; Playa de Las Arenas) presents a romantic picture, sitting on the headland with its billowing fishing nets and storm lamps, serving traditional Canarian and seafood.

Accommodation

Like many of Buenavista's best features, you have to work to find the **El Tejado Rural Hotel** (922 12 90 06; Bajada al campo de fútbol, 6; *www.el-tejado.es*) but you won't be disappointed with the reward; cottage-style rooms in an idyllic setting.

Fiestas

If you're in Buenavista at the same time as 1,500 head of cattle driven through the main street along with horses, goats, sheep and an assortment of pets including rabbit hutches on wheels and the occasional iguana or turkey on a lead...it must be **San Antonio Abad**.

Attractions

Buenavista Golf Course (*www.buenavistagolf.es*). Designed by Seve Ballesteros, this is an 18 hole, par 72 course with stunning views over the ocean to La Gomera. Some shots look as if you're about to drive straight into the sea and if your aim's as good as mine, which is why I'm not a golfer, that's exactly what you'll do.

Punta Teno Lighthouse. Drive to the most westerly point of the island via Nun's Point where, on breezy days, the wind threatens to carry you off the cliff face, and then through a tunnel roughly hewn through the seven million year old Teno Mountains, to emerge into a different climate zone. You'll find a small beach with views to Los Gigantes and crystal clear waters which seduce swimmers and divers alike. What you won't find is anywhere to buy lunch.

El Sauzal

Perched on the cliffs above the north coast, El Sauzal is home to some enchanting treasure troves. It also boasts one of the best views of Mount Teide on Tenerife.

Despite its diminutive size, the town played an important role in the history of the island. When disease ravished La Laguna, the island's council fled to El Sauzal, running Tenerife from the Iglesia de San Pedro Apóstol; a pristine, blindingly white structure with a Mudejar dome whose influence is more North African than European.

The town was on the stage coach route which transported travellers between the capital and La Orotava; waiting in El Sauzal for transport to take them to La Orotava, Isabel Lady Burton, wife of adventurer Sir Richard Burton, proclaimed her time there as "the happiest moment in my life".

El Sauzal possesses a tranquil charm, but apart from the eye-catching church opposite the town hall's trickling fountains, its most picturesque corners aren't immediately obvious. Signposted from the northern edge of town, Mirador La Garañona is a small park with walkways through tropical foliage and panoramic views of the cliffs and the north coast.

El Sauzal's jewel though is Parque Los Lavaderos, a former communal washing area below the church which has been turned into enchanting wild gardens with trickling springs. A bohemian, neo-hippy styled bar, 'Chocolate' overlooks the most magical area of the gardens and is the perfect location for a lazy Sunday afternoon, mulling over the crossword with a pot of infused jasmine tea.

Food

The stretch of road between El Sauzal and Tacoronte is renowned for having some of the best restaurants on Tenerife. Although none will disappoint, **Tacao** (922 56 41 73; Carretera General del Norte, 122) offers something slightly unusual; a German/Spanish fusion. Canarios love their grilled meats and sausages, so it's a marriage made in heaven. The best bit, if you're a real ale fan, is that the owner, Jochen brews speciality beers on the premises; the only establishment in Tenerife which does so.

El Sauzal

Accommodation

The 'Colonel's' is a real treasure. **Casa Adena** (656 67 65 16) in the scenic Los Angeles parish dates back to 1512 and has a pool designed by the Colonel's friend César Manrique. It's a wonderful hotchpotch of an old mansion

57

which would only suit those for whom character and atmosphere are more important than amenities.

Nightlife

El Sauzal Auditorio beside the town hall has a surprisingly varied programme which ranges from contemporary theatre and dance to rock bands and classical concerts.

Attractions

Tenerife's wine and honey museum is housed in the outbuildings of the appropriately rosé coloured **Casa del Vino 'La Baranda'** (signposted from the El Sauzal exit on the TF5). Most of the exhibits are in Spanish, but even if your grasp of the language doesn't stretch much beyond 'hola' it doesn't matter. La Baranda's photogenic rustic buildings and courtyards are a classic example of colonial architecture and worth a visit in their own right and anyway, there's a fabulous restaurant where the sensation on your taste buds transcends any language barrier.

DOWN UNDER IN TENERIFE

Living outside of your own country is never that simple. What could be more challenging than to live in a strange new land and foreign culture? While travellers have it easy, I think that it is particularly difficult for expatriates. Obviously the greater apart the host & donor countries, the harder it becomes.

In my case, I was born in Sydney and resided there for the next 27 years. Yet Tenerife is the opposite to Sydney in just about every respect. We drive on the wrong side of the road, the geography of the islands is totally different, the seasons are completely reversed and both places are at the antipode.

One of the most difficult things for any immigrant to deal with is making new friends or co-patriates. Being an Australian living in Tenerife, this is particularly difficult for me to cope with. Not counting my two cousins who were born in Australia and moved here as toddlers, I have met precisely *three* Australian citizens since I came here in late 2005. All three individuals who have decided to make Tenerife their home (at least for the foreseeable future) now speak fluent Spanish (myself included) and all three have integrated well as a result. I firmly believe that the only barrier to learning a language is your own desire or reluctance to do so.

My own personal story is quite simple. I came to this island in late 2005 after meeting a Canarian woman. Another one of my motives for coming here was the intention of starting some sort of cycling-related business. During the winter when the rest of Europe experiences much colder temperatures, Tenerife retains its Mediterranean climate and therefore becomes one of the best places for amateur and professional cyclists to train. The road up to Izaña, at an altitude of 2300m, is higher than any point in Australia. Being a keen cyclist, I saw that as a big opportunity.

For the first two years after moving to the North of Tenerife, I felt extremely 'displaced' - almost every single day. Even after 3 years, I continue feeling somewhat 'lost' here. Like neither is my home and yet they both are, all at the same time. I found myself analysing why I am here and if I made the right choice. The thought - or rather the temptation - of going back haunts me all the time.

The major problem for me is that Tenerife is an extremely small island compared with Australia. 4000 times smaller to be exact. In Australia, we leave vast tracts of land untouched. Here the land is constantly tended, tweaked and re-worked. Everywhere I look I see relentless construction all over the island. So I'm much more aware of these changes and their effect on this whole planet.

Lately, things seem so artificial, I've had the distinct feeling that I'm living in captivity in Tenerife, a bit like a goldfish living in an extra large goldfish bowl. Because of that, I have developed a pretty strong sense of agoraphobia; every time I travel down the same road, it reinforces how trapped I feel here. The only place I can find refuge is within the forest surrounding Mt Teide National Park. Although there's also the sense that everything has become familiar, so I definitely feel protected within a strange sort of comfort zone.

On this island, there are generally no trees below about 1000m. But you can't set about planting trees everywhere because that's not the way Canarians would have it (it creates too much shade for their food crops). And trying to change them is no easier than trying to change your own society.

On a more positive note, life is somehow more simple now; for me it's a bit like going back in time 10 years. For example, you can walk onto a bus or into a bank and there are no plastic security screens. And when you ring up an organisation, you are able to talk with a person straight away, not merely a computer.

People definitely have more contact with each other and they're not so much living on the edge of their breaking point. I suspect that I was escaping the stressful city life in Sydney more than anything else. Perhaps I would have been better off if I had have chosen to move to a country town and opted for a change in career instead of moving to the other side of the world.

I think I have become a richer person, but obviously not in the monetary sense. In fact I read somewhere that Australians were the third richest expatriates in the world. The one exception? Australian expatriates living in Spain did not earn anywhere near the other groups that were surveyed. Reading that did nothing to boost my confidence for a financially brighter future. Who knows, maybe I'll be the exception to the exception, but somehow I doubt it.

Dr. Leslie Brown,
www.tenerife-training.net / Tenerife-News-Cycling-Blog

Garachico

Garachico, once Tenerife's richest town, encapsulates Tenerife's boom and bust fortunes. Occupying a semicircular promontory on the north west coast it has been the victim of plague, floods, fires and pestilence. In 1706, Montaña Negra blew its top sending rivers of lava through the streets filling its deep-water harbour and robbing Garachico of its position as gateway to the Americas and Tenerife's premier port.

However disaster after disaster wasn't enough to break the town's spirit. Each time Mother Nature threw her worst, Garachico rose defiantly like a phoenix from the flames, and the townsfolk adopted the motto 'Glorious in Adversity'. The unluckiest town on Tenerife is also one of the most picturesque and, despite being destroyed many times over, one of the best preserved historical towns on the Canary Islands; hardly changing in size since the 16th century...maybe its tragic past deters more people from settling there.

Ironically Garachico's lava filled seafront has made it a popular destination for daytime visitors on coach excursions, many of whom don't venture onto its historic streets, where its true charms lie.

In its halcyon days, the town was home to wealthy merchants, bankers, artists, musicians and religious brotherhoods from Spain, Italy and Portugal. Their legacy is quaint cobbled streets lined with an eclectic mix of smart townhouses, churches, monasteries, convents and fishermens' cottages with terracotta and amber façades.

Plaza de la Libertad is arguably Tenerife's prettiest square. The bandstand kiosk and café, shaded by Indian laurels and complete with ubiquitous domino playing locals, is perfectly placed to soak up architectural delights such as the 16th century Moorish styled Iglesia de Nuestra Señora de Los Ángeles; the neoclassical town hall and the Iglesia de Santa Ana.

In Parque Puerta Tierra, built around an old toll gate (the only survivor of the original harbour), shaded paths wind through palm, fig and laurel trees.

Hidden amongst the undergrowth are 'poet's corner' (good luck trying to find anything that rhymes with 'there was a young man from Garachico...'), a traditional wooden 'lagar' (winepress) and busts of eminent townspeople. The park culminates at a vantage point with views across the town's red tiled rooftops and of the two slate coloured lava streams which forged Garachico's destiny.

A statue of a fellow in an oversized pith helmet on the town's northern edge pays homage to the night in 1666 when the townsfolk, weary of the English monopoly over the control of wine prices, broke into the wine cellars and smashed the lot, turning Garachico's streets red.

Beaches

The small pebble beach beside the harbour doesn't have any facilities and isn't the most comfortable for sunbathing, but its aquamarine waters are sheltered, attracting Spanish families who camp on the beach at weekends during the summer months.

Food

Most restaurants and cafés are situated along the town's seafront. Because of their vantage point, prices can be higher than those found in the streets behind the town's main façade.

At **Los Pinos** (922 83 01 34; C/Pérez Zamora, 6) the emphasis is on serving the sort of food they'd eat themselves rather than smart décor. It's a typically unfussy, rustic establishment where portions are enormous, the *chuletos de cerdo* (pork chops) look like they've been cut from a mutant sized pig and the wine from their own harvest is dangerously drinkable.

Casa Ramon (922 83 12 77; C/Esteban de Ponte, 2) is small, dark and with a limited menu which consists of whatever fresh meat and fish are available that day. It's owned by the mayor's mother, who fusses over you as if you were her own, guaranteeing authentic home cooking.

In a wonderful location beside the main square, service can be leisurely at **Aristides** (699 66 22 20; C/ Martín de Andujar, 1); however, its fresh fish and seafood dishes are worth waiting for. The *hueva de bacalao* (cod's roe) is something of an acquired taste and aesthetically, looking like skinned testicles in clear soup, it isn't the most attractive of dishes.

Accommodation

The **San Roque Hotel** (922 13 34 35; C/Esteban de Ponte, 32; *www.hotelsanroque.com*) is a renovated 18th century mansion with 20 rooms set around an inner courtyard. Whilst the architecture belongs to another century, the décor and furnishings are undisputedly contemporary, blending perfectly with dark polished balconies in the tranquil courtyard; it's exquisitely luxurious.

La Quinta Roja (922 13 33 77; Glorieta de San Francisco, 2; *www.quintaroja.com*); is a beautiful 16th century building with delightful courtyard, tasteful modern furnishings and its own wine bar. Standards aren't quite as high as the San Roque, but that's like saying a Bentley's not quite as good as a Rolls Royce.

Both hotels epitomise irresistible style and impeccable good taste and are perfect for the traveller who really does mean it when they say they want to get away from it all.

If you don't have the coffers to indulge in one of the above, **Pension Jardín** (922 83 02 45; C/Esteban de Ponte, 6; *www.argonautas.org*) in a 17th century townhouse is atmospheric, clean and friendly, though most rooms aren't en suite.

Nightlife

There's no nightlife to speak of and the few bars are very traditional; small and full of local men.

Fiestas

Garachico's streets flow with wine again during the **Romería de San Roque** on the 16th August, but that's only because so much gets spilled. Ox drawn carts trundle through the narrow streets followed by donkeys, goats and traditional musicians. Lads and lassies in traditional costume hand out gofio cakes, *papas arrugadas*, skewers of *carne fiesta* (seasoned pork kebabs) and steaks as well as gallons of wine from plastic flagons. Be wary of standing at a corner; these huge oxen are like Japanese super tankers and take a bit of stopping, there's a danger of being skewered as their handlers try to make them change course. If arriving by car, park as soon as you see other people parking theirs. Even though you might be a couple of kilometres from your destination; it's a sure sign that from here on in spaces are at a premium.

Garachico - Hotel La Quinta Roja

Attractions

In a wonderful example of triumph over adversity, the cause of the town's downfall has been transformed into its greatest attraction. **El Caletón** runs most of the length of the seafront and is a series of natural pools and channels in the lava; some are suitable for paddling, some deep enough for the town's *muchachos* to plunge into from great heights...well from about 10 feet, but it seems much higher when you're up there. A concrete path laid into the lava leads to secret corners and other pools. Because the lava protects the pools from the sea, bathing is possible most of the time, except when there are particularly rough seas in winter.

If the sense of history on Garachico's streets isn't enough, the **Castillo San Miguel** has detailed displays about the town's past whilst the former **Convento de San Francisco** has a few exhibits and a pleasant courtyard. The **Museo Carpinteria** is a hybrid of woodwork museum, wine shop and bar which also sells goatskin water flasks (useful for storing wine during fiestas).

Icod de los Vinos

Located a few kilometres inland, the town of Icod de los Vinos sits beneath the spectacular frames of Mount Teide and Pico Viejo in a lush valley dotted with plots of vines supported on frameworks of spindly branches. The town is famous for being home to one of the oldest living things on the planet, the Millennium Drago Tree, aged somewhere between 650 and 1,000 years. Legend has it that Atlas slew a multi headed dragon in the Garden of Hespérides (Tenerife) and a tree with multitudinous crowns sprang up from every drop of spilled dragon blood. This impressive specimen stands in the centre of landscaped gardens (€4 entrance) and whilst they're pleasant enough for a stroll, the best view of the tree is actually from the main square which overlooks them.

> *"The Drago tree is more than just a Tenerife icon, it is one of the oldest living members of the plant kingdom and its history has as many facets as the tree has crowns; a tangled tale of idolatry, exploitation and magic."*
> **'A Dragon's Tale' special feature**
> March 2007 issue of Living Tenerife magazine (www.livingtenerife.com)

The most attractive part of town begins at the jacaranda shaded plaza beside the Iglesia de San Marcos and leads through the picturesque Plaza de la Pila surrounded by 16th, 17th and 18th century houses with carved wooden balconies. Heading inwards involves tackling ridiculously steep streets, but a short, lung expanding ascent along C/San Antonio rewards intrepid visitors with a second ancient drago.

The old town is linked with the new by C/San Sebastián which has pavement cafes, chic independent clothes and artisan jewellery shops.

Beaches

It's only a hop, skip and a jump to San Marcos on Icod's coast. The black sand, sheltered bay is backed on one side by unattractive apartment blocks, but it's favoured by locals and has a couple of restaurants where you can partake of the local white wine with fried sea bass.

Food

Restaurants almost exclusively serve traditional Canarian cuisine. Specialities include *cabrito* (kid) and *bacalao en escabeche* (cod in brine).

Accommodation

A real shortage of places to stay short term; limited to a few Casas Rurales.

Fiestas

On the 29th November the new wines are ready for quaffing and bodegas throw open the doors of their wine cellars. In the past barrels were transported from the upper town to the sea by wooden sleds. As streets are almost vertical, this was a bit 'Wages of Fear' and a precarious business. Nowadays the tradition has evolved into an extreme sport worthy of 'Jackass'. The *'arrastre de las tablas'* involves streets being barricaded with mountains of tyres so that fearless, or wine fuelled, local lads who come screaming down them on tiny wooden sleds have a safety barrier to crash into at the bottom. C/del Plano is a good place to enjoy the best of the mayhem.

Attractions

El Mariposario (*www.mariposario.com*) is a wonderful butterfly garden whose owners are committed to conservation and creating the perfect environment for their flamboyant *'mariposas'* to thrive. Unfortunately the local council don't share the same values and the park is constantly under threat of closure because of petty politics.

If claustrophobia isn't a problem take a trip to the dark side with a two-hour guided exploration of **La Cueva del Viento** (*www.cuevadelviento.net*). The 17km volcanic tube is the longest in Europe.

La Laguna

One of the Canary Island's most interesting cities, San Cristóbal de La Laguna is often overlooked by visitors; probably because it doesn't have a beach and from the northern TF5 motorway which runs parallel to the city it looks like an unattractive concrete jungle.

But the urban 20th century façade hides a real gem of an historic city centre. Perfectly preserved streets and squares are lined with colonial 16th, 17th and 18th century mansions designed by Genovese, French, Portuguese, Castilian and Flemish architects; earning it UNESCO World Heritage status.

Situated inland 600 metres above sea level (making it considerably cooler than coastal communities) in the Aguere Valley at the gateway to the Anaga Mountains, La Laguna was founded in 1496 by Tenerife's conqueror, Fernández de Lugo. Its location was chosen for strategic purposes; being inland it was safe from attacks from the sea, especially from corsairs who terrorised the islands, and it had a lagoon to provide vital water supplies.

The city was Tenerife's original capital and as the biggest settlement in the Canary Islands, attracted wealthy noblemen, merchants and professionals. Where the money went, so did religious orders and La Laguna became the archipelago's ecclesiastical centre and a seat of learning; the University of La Laguna was founded in 1742.

The city's layout, based around a series of squares in grid format, was groundbreaking for its time and became the blueprint for many Latin American cities.

In 1821, the port of Santa Cruz became Tenerife's capital and in 1837 the lagoon was drained after deforestation had resulted in it becoming stagnant and a source of disease.

It's a city for travellers rather than casual tourists and the best way to get to know it is to pick up a '*mapa turístico*' from the tourist information office in the Casa de los Capitanes (C/Obispo Rey, beside Plaza del Adelantado) and set off to explore its cobbled streets lined by smart mansions and convents with towers whose latticed wooden balconies enabled cloistered nuns to see without being seen. Detours into churches and inviting doorways reveal tranquil leafy courtyards and curios like the baptismal font used to baptise the Guanche in the Iglesia de la Concepción, or the skull and crossbones engraved into the stone floor of the Iglesia de Santo Domingo.

Having a university lends the city a cosmopolitan air of sophistication, and stylish students share cobble space with old men in fedoras and nuns in slate grey habits. Shops are similarly contrasting; musty bookshops, barbers with lumbering antique chairs and *tabacs* whose walls are steeped with the aroma of tobacco leaf sit comfortably beside chic shops displaying the latest catwalk fashions.

69

Plaza del Adelantado was the once focal point of the old city, but since the relocation of the agricultural market (great place for spices, salted fish and exhibition worthy vegetables) to Plaza del Cristo, the plaza has lost some of its vibrancy; however the benches around its wonderful Carrara marble fountain are still an unbeatable spot for soaking up the charm of this living open air museum.

Food

Atmospheric and inviting eateries are conveniently dotted around the old streets; however, apart from the few with tables and chairs outside, they're not always easy to spot.

Patio Canario (922 26 46 57; C/Manuel de Ossuna, 8) has rustic décor, chunky tables and, importantly a bright, covered courtyard which means that it's possible to pick at their homemade tapas and sausages whatever La Laguna's temperamental weather is doing.

Iberian hams are the speciality at **La Parroquía** (922 25 60 57; C/ Bencomo, 38) opposite the perennially 'under renovation' cathedral. It's cosy and suitably ecclesiastical in style with a good selection of traditional meat and fish dishes.

The South American influence is strong in the city and there are a few good *areperas* around. **La Perla del Caribe** (Plaza del Adelantado) has a terrible name and looks nondescript; but their *arepas* are stonkingly good, especially the *'reina'* (chicken and avocado) and the *'carne mechado'* (spiced meat).

Accommodation

It's interesting to note that in the mid 19th century there were 6 inns in La Laguna. Today, when the number of annual visitors to Tenerife reaches into the millions, there are only two, with a third planned.

It's only 2 stars, but the 18th century **Hotel Aguere** (922 25 94 90; C/la Carrera, 55; *www.hotelaguere.es*) oozes bags more character than any number of modern 5 stars. Rooms are clean, but basic and set around a wonderful marble tiled courtyard with a coffee shop where it's possible to imagine any number of brief encounters taking place.

The apartments of the **Hotel Nivaria** (922 26 40 52; *www.hotelnivaria.com*) are located in a converted 17th century mansion overlooking Plaza del Adelantado. The building is charming and it's in a fantastic location in the heart of the old quarter, even if the décor of the communal areas and in the clean, spacious apartments is uninspiring.

Nightlife

Being a university city means you can be sure of one thing; a vibrant nightlife. You wouldn't know it during the day, but by midnight, the triangle of streets in the newer part of the city between the Central Campus and Plaza San Cristóbal explode into life. Groups of students, blessed with that Spanish knack of effortlessly looking cool, down a couple of *combinados* (usually rum and coke) on their wrought iron balconies, before heading to the throng of bars below, where house, Latino and jazz vibes vie for dominance.

Bars in the old quarter are much more sedate and spread out; a mix of traditional haunts with narrow Andalusian doorways and comfortably bohemian café bars which look as though they could be someone's living room.

Throughout the year, concerts featuring international as well as Spanish bands are held in the plaza in front of the University Campus.

Alternatively, a slice of culture in an old fashioned grandiose setting can be experienced at the lovingly restored **Teatro Leal**, recently re-opened after 17 years.

Fiestas

It's impossible not to associate the hooded outfits with the Ku Klux Klan who corrupted the image, but the scarlet, emerald and purple cloths which hide the identities of those participating in the **Semana Santa** (Easter) processions were designed to allow devout Catholics to show penitence anonymously. The two main processions are the 'Magna' and the 'Silent Procession' at 17.00 and 21.00 respectively on *Viernes Santos* (Good Friday) when brotherhood after brotherhood solemnly parade through the old streets, some carrying full sized crucifixes. The afternoon procession is best for photographs, but the candlelit 'Silent Procession' probably shades it in terms of atmosphere. It might be Tenerife's quietest celebrations, but it's the most evocative; once witnessed, never forgotten.

Attractions

The **Instituto Cabrero Pinto** (C/San Agustín, 48) is a perfect example of La Laguna's seamless integration of the contemporary with the historic. The former 16th century convent now houses art galleries with *avant garde* 21st century exhibitions. Its profuse courtyard garden underneath a carved tea wood balcony is a perfect spot for contemplation (i.e. trying to figure out what the exhibits actually mean).

Displays and information at the **History Museum** (C/San Agustín, 22) might be on the 'abridged' side, but it's another beautiful building worth exploring.

Nature and science are the themes at the **(MCC) Museum of Science and the Cosmos** (C/La Vía Láctea; *www.museosdetenerife.org*); 100 interactive exhibits turn potentially dry subjects into family friendly ones. (Entrance to Museums on Tenerife is free on Sundays).

La Orotava

Arrive at the bus station or drive in from the TF5 and you'll find yourself in the middle of a busy, unappealing sprawl of spare parts outlets and hardware shops wondering why on earth anyone would recommend this place.

But make your way to the primrose walls of the 17th century Iglesia de San Agustín on Carrera de Escultor Estevez and you're at the start of the old quarter where beautifully preserved 16th, 17th and 18th century mansions line elegant cobbled streets and the trees outnumber the lamp posts.

Between 300 and 400 metres above sea level in the valley from which it derived its name, La Orotava is the jewel in Tenerife's crown.

Considered the most perfect location on Tenerife by the conquering Fernández de Lugo, lands here were at a premium when it came to handing them out as booty in reward for financing the conquest. Thus La Orotava established itself as home to the island's aristocracy and still maintains its aristocratic air today.

The atmosphere in the heart of the old town is that of quiet sophistication and affluence with upmarket independent shops selling books, antiques and ornaments and chic tascas tucked into leafy courtyards.

Unsurprisingly, for a town set into the sides of a valley, its streets are steep and wandering around for a day will make itself known to your calves. It's also a busy working town, so outside of siesta hours roads are constantly busy and crossing them can be a dodgy business.

At this height above sea level the air is a good bit chillier than at the coast, so in winter bring something warm to put on.

Accommodation

You won't find any modern, high-rise hotels in La Orotava. Here the discerning traveller disappears behind an unassuming exterior to emerge into the tranquil courtyard of a rural hotel where traditional carved wooden balconies and 17th century tiles abound and their idea of facilities is a telephone in your room.

Right in the heart of the old town, **Hotel Rural Victoria** (922 33 16 83; Hermano Apolinar, *8*; *www.hotelruralvictoria.com*) offers style, elegance and excellent cuisine in a 300 year old mansion.

Big on history but small on space and natural light is the 16th century **Hotel Rural Orotava** (922 32 27 93; Calle Escultor Estevez, 17; *www.saborcanario.net*); a traditional Canarian mansion.

Exquisite en suite bathrooms are one of the selling points at **Hotel Alhambra** (922 32 04 34; C/Nicandro González Borges, 19; *www.alhambra-teneriffa.com*). An 18th century mansion restored in Arabic style with just 5 individually styled double rooms.

Food

Sabor Canario (922 32 27 93; Carrera 17-23*)* has traditional Canarian cuisine specialising in grilled meats in the atmospheric courtyard of the Hotel Rural Orotava.

La Duquesa (922 63 69 02; Pl. Patricio García, 6) is a small, friendly restaurant by the side of Iglesia Concepción. Traditional food, big portions, great value.

Kiú (922 32 37 38; Colegio, 7; *www.zonakiu.net*) has contemporary style and great food in the stunning surroundings of Casa Lercaro. Something for the weekend perhaps?

Liceo de Taoro (922 33 01 19; Plaza de la Constitución; *www.liceodetaoro.es*) has a good, basic Canarian menu del día in the poshest building in town for just €12 a head.

Nightlife

La Canela behind Iglesia San Agustín is a popular café bar and has a range of live music from folk to rock. **Añepa** *www.pubañepa.es* on Calle Rosales is an intimate courtyard corner with art exhibitions and regular live music, and for dance addicts **La Basilica** *www.nuevabasilica.com* on the Poligono Industrial Estate just off the TF5 provides fixes of House and Latino with live bands on Friday nights.

Fiestas

The Flower Carpets of Corpus Christi are exquisite, transient works of art which only exist for a few short hours and should be on every respectable traveller's list of 'must sees'.

On the feast of Corpus Christi, the town takes on a carnival atmosphere as the streets around Iglesia de la Concepción are decorated in elaborately designed carpets of petals. In the immense plaza that fronts the Town Hall, an 850 sq metre tapestry is created from coloured soils and sand taken from the Teide National Park. The tapestry is the largest of its kind in the world and is nothing less than breathtaking in its intricacy and composition.

That same evening, the Corpus Christi procession walks over them all on its way to the church.

To get the best of the carpets, arrive around midday on the day, late enough so that designs will be well under way but early enough to give yourself time for at least a couple of circuits. At the Town Hall, go inside and upstairs to one of the balconies that overlook the plaza for a perfect shot.

And if you really want to see something special, go along to the Town Hall the day before to see the master *alfombristas* (carpet makers) at work, it's like watching Michelangelo paint the Sistine Chapel... well, it's brilliant anyway.

An alfombrista (carpet maker) at work for Corpus Christi

The Romería de San Isidro is one of the biggest and best on Tenerife. The entire town dress in traditional *mago* costumes and take to the streets in a procession to celebrate their Saint's feast day.

Beginning with camels ridden by the *Romería* Queens, the old town's narrow main street witnesses no less than 70 decorated carts pulled by oxen, each one packed to the gunwales with laughing people, a barbecue on which an assortment of prime cuts are being roasted and a couple of barrels of *vino del país*, or country wine. Accompanying the carts are bands of musicians *(parrandas)* and troupes of traditional dancers.

This is a boisterous, three to four hour marathon that involves a great deal of standing around so 'sensible' shoes are well, sensible. The idea is to share in the town's bountiful harvest by accepting the food and wine being handed down to you from the carts, it's positively rude to refuse.

Buy yourself a small glass which hangs in a leather pouch around your neck (on sale from *vaso* vendors on the day) and enjoy. Who *says* there's no such thing as a free lunch?

Attractions

Casas de Los Balcones are the finest examples of traditional balconied houses to be found on Tenerife and so attract large numbers of tour groups. Luckily, they tend to confine themselves to the Casa del Turista which is really just a front for souvenir selling.

Across the road is the infinitely lovelier and quieter Casa Méndez-Fonseca. Head inside to its stunning courtyard and fork out the pittance entrance fee to explore its quirky museum upstairs.

Leave the tour groups behind altogether and drop down Calle Colegio to find Casa Lercaro with its beautiful exterior, its stunning balconied interior courtyard and its "how much do you want for the lot?" shop upstairs.

Just a few steps further down Colegio takes you to the **Iglesia de la Concepción**; an 18th century Baroque masterpiece with a rainbow coloured dome and twin towers which are an icon of La Orotava's skyline.

For nature lovers the 18th century formal Italian **Victoria Gardens** are pristine and are graced with a marble mausoleum. They're also well worth seeing at dusk when up-lighting gives the park a distinctly 'Strictly Ballroom' look. On the wilder side, the **Botanical Gardens**, little sister to the one in Puerto de la Cruz, is a mini jungle of exotic plant life with a mystical Drago tree at its centre.

77

A KILLER VIEW

From my vantage point on the Town Hall's balcony, I had a bird's eye view of the vast tapestry in the plaza below me. At its centre was an intricately detailed depiction of 'The Good Samaritan' and surrounding it were evocative images alluding to the plight of our African neighbours. The message was clear.

Fear, anxiety and compassion had been captured on the faces in the broad tableau. It was a masterpiece and what made it truly incredible was that it hadn't been created with paints and brushes, but with sand from Las Cañadas del Teide. The main sand tapestry showpiece of the Corpus Christi celebrations in La Orotava, when the streets are carpeted with floral images, was also the biggest of its kind in the world – official.

I focused my camera, vaguely aware of a change in tone from the other admirers around me. It took a couple of seconds before I realised that the *'oohs'* and *'aahs'* had changed to shouts of *'assassin'* and *'murderer'*. I turned to see what was going on and discovered to my horror that the accusing cries were directed at me.

Just my luck that on a day I'd casually thrown on a T-shirt with Che Guevara's face plastered across it, I would run into a group of exiled Cubans living in Miami who'd fled from Che and his mate Fidel during the Cuban revolution and who happened to be visiting Tenerife for Corpus Christi. As the men in the septuagenarian group surrounded me and the women broke down in tears at the very sight of the 'assassin' on my chest, the accusations came thick and fast – *"Murderer! He shot my father"*, *"He wanted me dead; I barely escaped Cuba with my life"*.

I stood, mouth gaping like the Grand Canyon, completely bemused, whilst the group's American guide apologised profusely for the verbal assault. I was only half listening as I had one eye on the security guards who had shuffled closer, clearly unsure of what action, if any, they should take. I decided to take the decision out of their hands and that the most sensible course of action was to do a 'Jason Bourne' and blend anonymously back into the thousands of people who were lining La Orotava's picturesque streets to see the town's famous floral carpets, leaving my accusers to their grief.

La Orotava's flower carpets are a beautiful and unforgettable sight and I'd strongly recommend that anyone who's on Tenerife during Corpus Christi should heed the words written over 150 years ago by historian, Sabino Bethelot:

"...today, the town of La Orotava blossoms. You shouldn't miss it."

Just don't wear a T-shirt with a picture of Che Guevara printed on it.

Jack Montgomery, co-author 'Going Native Tenerife'

Los Realejos

The conquest of Tenerife ended in Los Realejos when the Guanche Menceys (kings) surrendered and were baptised into Christianity. It was here, below the lush forested slopes of the Tigaiga Mountain range, that Tenerife's conqueror, Fernández de Lugo, made his home.

"Los Realejos...is rarely on a tourist map, yet it holds a significant place in Tenerife's history. It was here that the last of the native Guanche Menceys (Kings) surrendered to the Spanish in 1496, thus relinquishing Tenerife into Spanish domain."
'Island Drives – the definitive guide to exploring Tenerife by car' *www.realtenerifeislanddrives.com*

Realejos has two centres, Bajo near the TF5 motorway and Alto, a few hundred, muscle torturing metres higher up the valley. Whilst many of its older buildings were destroyed by fire over the centuries, there are still enough historic corners to warrant a visit. Tenerife's oldest church, the **Iglesia de Santiago Apóstal** in Realejos Alto, has a spire straight out of Hans Christian Anderson. Fernández de Lugo's former abode, the Hacienda de los Principes, can be found in Realejos Bajo near an unusual pair of drago trees, Los Gemelos (the twins).

Exploring Los Realejos can be frustrating; parking is almost impossible and the one-way system is bewildering, but it exudes a bustling charm. While it's not an ideal choice for a package holiday, it will suit travellers seeking a taste of Tenerife's history.

Beaches

El Socorro, a few kilometres from town, is a beautiful black sand beach with lifeguard, toilet facilities and a wonderful little fish restaurant. The beach shelves gently into waves which reach a height of five metres in winter, making it a favourite spot with surfers.

Food

The great and the good of Tenerife travel to dine at **El Monasterío** (922 34 43 11; La Montañeta). Set in the grounds of an immaculately renovated monastery on a volcanic cone there are five restaurants to choose from. A romantic option is to indulge in a champagne breakfast; at around €9 a head, it's a bit of affordable decadence.

Accommodation

Choices in town are limited to a couple of Casa Rurales. The closest hotel is the **Tierra de Oro** (922 34 12 13; La Cartaya; *www.hotelspatierradeoro.com*) which has excellent spa facilities.

Nightlife

A few quiet bars and no clubs, but with 80 fiestas, short film seasons, jazz weekends, world music festivals and cinema on the beach taking place throughout the year, who needs them.

Fiestas

Los Realejos claims to celebrate more fiestas than any other place in Spain. It's home to the Toste Brothers' Pyrotechnics factory, suppliers of fireworks all over the Canary Islands, which might explain why there's such a penchant for fiestas.

The most explosive is celebrated on 3rd May when crosses throughout the town are elaborately decorated and a three-hour firework display lights up the skies above the town.

The plaza in front of the town hall is a good spot to enjoy the spectacle, which starts from around 10.00pm. The display isn't continuous and it can be a bit nippy; a jacket is essential. In recent years the international paragliding festival, **FLYPA** has been incorporated into the celebrations.

Attractions

An old merchants' trail, on the coast below Los Realejos, leads from the **San Pedro Mirador** past banana plantations, haciendas, secret coves and palm groves to a tiny fort, where soldiers used to keep a vigil for pirates. It's an absolutely delightful spot and feels more Caribbean than Canary Islands.

Los Silos

Hitherto a stranger to guide books, the low rise white buildings and icing sugar-coated spire of the church of Los Silos snuggle in a fertile green carpet known as Isla

Baja at the foot of the Teno Mountains on Tenerife's north west coast.

At its heart, the laurel shaded plaza plays host to architecture spanning four centuries, a church whose name, *La Iglesia de La Luz* (Church of the Light) is a descriptor as well as a title and a beautifully restored 17th century former convent.

It's a picturesque village, full of character and protected from the attentions of tour groups by virtue of its narrow streets which prohibit access by buses.

Populated since before the conquest due to the natural fertility of the area, Los Silos grew cereals, sugar cane and vines which it transported to neighbouring Garachico for export. The village is actually named after three large grain silos built in the 15th century to store the abundant crop.

Today its tradition of agriculture continues and the area is one of the main suppliers of organic produce on the island.

At its coastal development of El Puertito is a former sugar refinery, now a banana storage warehouse, to which much of the surrounding forest was sacrificed in the 16th century. There's also a small telegraph station built to receive Tenerife's first electronic communication cable which was laid underwater from La Palma in 1883. A recent addition to the coastal scenery is the 16 metre long, over 20 tonnes in weight skeleton of a whale; a monument to man's relationship with the sea.

Beaches

Although it has plenty of coastline, Los Silos has no beaches. Instead there are a couple of natural rock pools which are popular in summer, and the rest of the year the El Piscina complex in El Puertito has an Olympic-sized swimming pool, sun-bathing terraces and a kiddies area.

Food

Typically Canarian dishes tend to dominate the no frills cafes and restaurants around town but the real culinary delight of Los Silos is the **El Aderno** (922 12 73 68; C/El Olivo, 1; *www.eladerno.com*) bakery and chocolate cave where the cakes and home made choccies will bring on dieting amnesia and replace it with sugar-induced euphoria.

Accommodation

A smattering of rural houses around the area offer style and rustic charm while **Casa Amarilla**, the 18th century former home of the sugar refinery manager (607 46 84 45; La Caleta de Interián; *www.fincacasamarilla.com*) in La Caleta provides an elegant base from which to explore the area.

Nightlife

The **La Cúpula** disco and karaoke bar in the El Piscina complex (*www.discopublacupula.com*) can legitimately advertise itself as the *only* place to go in the Isla Baja area. Unsurprisingly, it gets busy.

Fiestas

Early December sees fairytale figures, giant spiders and various 'Grimm' characters decorating the Plaza and the Convent of San Sebastián as Los Silos plays host to one of Tenerife's most unusual festivals. The *Festival Internacional Del Cuento* (International Storytelling Festival) attracts children from across the island to lend their ears and their imaginations to storytellers from all corners of the globe. After dark, the tales grow more eerie and erotic as the adult folk stories unfold to tickle the goosebumps ...and the parts other stories cannot reach.

Puerto de la Cruz

Puerto de la Cruz, on the north coast, is the only town on Tenerife which has both the amenities of a tourist resort and is resolutely Canarian in character. Originally the port for La Orotava, the town's fortune changed in 1706 when an eruption ended Garachico's reign as Tenerife's main port and almost overnight, Puerto became an outlet for the area's exports.

"On the left lies the little flat town of the Puerto, over which in clear weather the Island of La Palma emerges from its mantle of clouds, and many a gorgeous sunset bathes the whole town in a mist of rosy light, recalling the legend that in days of old, navigators had christened the little fishing-port the Puerto de Oro..."

**Florence Du Kane on Puerto de la Cruz,
'The Canary Islands' published 1911**

For centuries its location at the foot of the Orotava Valley attracted scientists, explorers and authors (Agatha Christie set her short story 'The Man from the Sea' in Puerto). Nowadays Northern Europeans escaping dreary winters and seeking a dose of culture as well as warm weather boost the population between November and April. During the summer months Spanish mainlanders descend en masse adding a 24/7 *joie de vivre* to the town's streets.

Puerto's heart lies in the squares and cobbled streets of the old town. Wander along the harbour during early morning as fishermen bring their catches ashore and elderly gents in fedoras play cards loudly, or through Plaza del Charco at dusk when families from grandmothers to toddlers congregate to socialise and it won't take long to discover what sets Puerto apart from other resorts.

Beaches

The César Manrique designed black sand beach of Playa Jardín stretches from the Castillo San Felipe to Punta Brava. Brits and Germans use the sunbeds at the rear of the beach; Spanish decamp on the sand closer to the shoreline. Waves here can pack a punch; great fun for fearless swimmers, less so if you lack confidence in the water.

At the eastern end of town, Playa Martiánez is a smaller black sand beach mostly favoured by surfers.

Puerto de la Cruz packed during Fiesta de la Virgen del Carmen

The real 'get away from it all' beaches are three coves at Playa Bollullo, accessed via a path from La Paz district. The main beach has a lifeguard and a great little bar overlooking the beach; the others are popular for nude sunbathing and surfing or, if you're really adventurous, both.

Food

With over a hundred restaurants, there's something to suit all palates. The best area for dining is the Ranilla district where trendy new restaurants and bars have sprung up beside cat's face cottages.

Tasquita de Min (922 37 18 34; C/Mesquinez) has fresh marine inspired décor and is packed out daily with locals. Order Tenerife's favourite fish dish, the *vieja* (parrot fish) and discover why. Their *lapas* (limpets in coriander and garlic sauce) are also to die for.

For an authentic tapas experience try one of the bars at the top of C/Perdomo. If squeezing in amongst grizzled and slightly sozzled fishermen sounds a tad too authentic, **Cha Paula** (922 38 07 30; C/Blanco, 19) is also a fishermen's bar, but one with an adjoining rustic dining room and quaint courtyard; the *chipirones* (small squid) are the best in town.

Mil Sabores (922 36 81 72; C/Cruz Verde, 5) lives up to its name with a menu brimming with wonderfully inventive Mediterranean cuisine. The choice of mouth-watering dishes such as p*anga fish in a mango sauce* will have foodies in ecstasy.

Sophisticated, sexy and still somewhat of a rarity on Spanish soil, **El Maná** (922 36 85 23; C/Mesquinez, 23) has a menu consisting mainly of contemporary vegetarian dishes (there's a meat option – they're not daft). Stylish furnishings compliment equally stylish food. Order the *degustacion*, relax and let the chef seduce your taste-buds.

Accommodation

Five star hotels are about as common as designer clothes these days; however, the **Hotel Botanico** in La Paz (902 08 00 00; C/ Richard Yeoward 1;

www.hotelbotanico.com) is a throwback to the days when 5 stars guaranteed unadulterated luxury. The exquisite Oriental Spa garden is an added bonus.

Taoro is the town's most tranquil area with tropical gardens, water cascades, the former casino and the family run **Hotel Tigaiga** (922 38 35 00; Parque Taoro, 28; www.tigaiga.com) whose personal service and tastefully decorated rooms with great views earn it a loyal following.

Soak up some history at the **Hotel Monopol** (922 38 46 11; C/Quintana, 15; www.monopoltf.com) whose credentials as a hotel date back to 1881; great location opposite the picturesque Plaza Iglesia. Request a room in the old building; the newer annex is less charming.

There are modest pensions and small hotels like the **Puerto Azul** (922 38 32 13; C/del Lomo, 24; www.puerto-azul.com) in the Ranilla district which are available for longer term rent. It's an atmospheric area which still retains the flavour of the town's fishing port origins.

Nightlife

Plaza Charco is the place to chill early evening; it's a hive of bustling activity and the bars surrounding the plaza couldn't be better positioned for those with a passion for people watching.

Many locals don't come out to play until midnight when bars in the streets of the old town, especially around Calle Iriarte and along Calle La Hoya fill to near bursting point. The pick of these is **Azucar**; a vibrant Cuban bar in a former gentlemen's club. Mojitos flow like water and the mainly South American patrons break into elaborate and steamy salsa routines where they stand; it could easily be downtown Havana.

From 3.00am. onwards Avenida Generalisimo, home of Puerto's club and gay scene, bursts into life.

Fiestas

With fiestas of one sort or another taking place every month, from contemporary to celebrations steeped in Guanche tradition, Puerto lays claim to being the fiesta capital of Tenerife. The embarkation of the **Virgen del Carmen** during the July Fiestas and the beach party and goat bathing of the **Fiestas of San Juan** in June provide some of the most colourful pageants, but it's the town's **'Carnaval'** (Feb/March) which is the main extravaganza of the year.

A whirlwind week of flamboyant processions and surreal events includes the **'Burial of the Sardine'** and the **'Mascarita Ponte Tacon'** (an outrageous drag marathon not for the easily offended). The soul of Carnaval lies in the street parties which take place nightly around Plaza Charco. From midnight to dawn, thousands of revellers in fancy dress salsa their way through the streets. To really experience Carnaval, it's essential to dress up; it makes the world of difference.

Attractions

One of Tenerife's main tourist attractions is **Loro Parque** (*www.loroparque.com*). Set in lush tropical gardens, animal enclosures are spacious and designed to replicate their inhabitant's natural environment, although the parrots which first brought fame to the park have been somewhat relegated to a sideshow. Nowadays the main draws are the orca, dolphin and sea lion shows. A personal favourite is Planet Penguin; a simulated iceberg where it actually snows.

Jardín Botánico in La Paz (entrance €3), originally established as an acclimatisation garden for specimens en route to the mainland, is a lush 'Lost World' of giant strelitzias and emerald foliage. Leafy paths lead past lily ponds, and exotic plants like the 'drunken' and 'sausage' trees. It's a tranquil oasis to while away a few relaxing hours, but watch out for the ancient banyan which is said to eat tourists after dark.

A goat being bathed in the harbour for Fiesta de San Juan

Designed by César Manrique, **Costa Martiánez** (entrance and sunbed €3.50) is one part open air art gallery, three parts swimming pool complex. Abstract sculptures add a unique style to the plunge pools, Jacuzzis, children's and lake sized pools below towering palms which run almost the entire length of the town's promenade. After dark the town's casino, under the main pool, opens its doors for would be James Bonds.

YOU KNOW WHEN YOU'VE BEEN CARNAVAL-ED...

"I need some false breasts," said Martin, veering off towards Plaza Charco and the assortment of stalls bedecked with pirate hats, guns, sparkly wigs, stage make-up and of course, false boobs.

It had already been a long day. It was never going to be easy kitting out four teenagers and a mum and dad with enough outfits to get them through the entire week of Carnaval. Despite emails underlining the need to bring costumes with them, restrictive luggage allowances simply didn't permit such extravagances. Our long time friends Martin and Anne, their teenage son and daughter Dan and Grace and Dan and Grace's friends Leanne and Chris had come on holiday to Puerto de la Cruz to enjoy the spectacle we had told them so much about. Monday night spent partying in the streets until the early hours had served to underline our assurances that fancy dress was not optional if you really wanted to get the full 'Carnaval experience'.

So assorted costumes and props had been acquired during the morning; a monk's habit, two pairs of angel wings, a Bishop's cassock and mitre, Venetian face masks and several pairs of fishnet tights.

There was a particularly poignant moment for Anne when, emerging from a dress shop in town, she wiped an imaginary tear from her eye and said, *"It's such a proud moment when you buy your son his first little black dress."*

Ash Wednesday is 'Burial of the Sardine' night; traditionally the last night of Carnaval when the symbolic sardine is cremated to denote the demise of the festivities. Nowadays it marks the mid-way point in a week long party.

A giant papier mâché sardine is paraded through the streets of the town followed by hordes of wailing widows, most of them men, in full widow's weeds, hats, veils and the ubiquitous fishnets. Some of the 'widows' are so overcome by grief that they swoon at regular intervals during the procession, revealing naughty underwear and assorted sex toys tucked into frilly garters.

I think it's fair to say that, as we entered Plaza Charco to await the arrival of the cortège, we cut a dash.

Jack was wearing a blonde wig, balloons for boobs beneath a short, black, satin number of mine (long since despatched to the 'fancy dress' box), full make-up including scarlet lipstick, laddered black tights and his size 9 trainers. He had a sort of 'mad Scandinavian prostitute' look that surprised both of us.

Martin's false boobs were a triumph; one nipple peeped seductively from behind its black lace vest while the other brazenly exposed itself fully. The addition of a brown, curly wig, calf length tight skirt which he'd borrowed from me, fishnets and trainers completed the 'Barbara Woodhouse on mescalin' look.

A few beers were needed to loosen the nerves but by the time the sardine had been duly mourned then set alight amidst a kaleidoscopic explosion of fireworks and the party had moved to Plaza Charco to see in the dawn, the men seemed to slide further and further into character, camping it up like it was something they'd secretly fancied doing for years.

Come to think of it, where *is* that skirt I lent Martin...?

Andrea Montgomery, co-author
'Going Native in Tenerife'

Santa Úrsula

Set 300 metres above Tenerife's north coast a mere five minute drive from Puerto de la Cruz, Santa Úrsula is a small working town with a penchant for good food, the right soil and conditions for producing good wines and a surprisingly large British ex-pat population.

As recently as 50 years ago, this area was covered in palm groves, vines, bananas and fruit trees with just the church, parochial house and a few farmers' cottages to mark the position of the village. Today the Carretera Provincial which runs through its centre, linking the historic hill towns of the north from the old capital of La Laguna to La Orotava and Teide, is lined with a healthy selection of shops, family run restaurants and 'se vende vino' (wine for sale) signs from dozens of small harvests which occupy every inch of cultivated land.

Away from the main thoroughfare, streets climb steeply into the upper reaches of the village, making walking a sweaty business and parking a constant handbrake test and there are parts of the municipality that are simply no-go areas for anything other than a 4x4.

Beyond the north motorway, above the rocky coastline, is the residential area of La Quinta; a Legoland of pastel coloured housing estates which spread across the headland where once palm groves thrived.

Accommodation

Perched on the headland alongside the La Quinta development is the Spa Aparthotel **La Quinta Park** (922 30 09 51; Urbanizacion La Quinta s/n; *www.spalaquintapark.com*) where you can be pummelled and pampered whilst enjoying spectacular views over Tenerife's **tropical** north coast.

Food

One family dominates the best of the culinary offerings in Santa Úrsula, as anyone who lives there will testify. It all began in 1926 when Ceferina Martín and her Cuban husband opened what is today called '**La Bodeguita de Enfrente** (922 30 27 60; C/Provincial Cuesta, 130; *www.labodeguitadeenfrente.net*) to feed travellers en route to La Orotava and the peak. Today, her grandsons Mario, Xavier and Fabián have carried on the family tradition.

Donde Mario (922 30 45 85; C/Provincial Cuesta,199; *www.dondemario.net*) and **El Calderito** (922 30 19 18; C/Provincial Cuesta, 130; *www.elcalderitodelaabuela.net*) join La Bodeguita in providing excellent cuisine in elegantly rustic surroundings which imbue Santa Úrsula with a culinary pedigree way beyond its size. And they're a well kept secret, or at least, they were until now.

Nightlife

Nightlife is mainly provided by dropping down the hill into Puerto de la Cruz, but for an early evening warm up session, head to '**Africa**' on the main street where the décor and ambience only lack the occasional Masai warrior propping up the bar to have you believing you've hopped the 300 km to the real thing.

Attractions

When in 1799 Alexander von Humboldt stood in Santa Úrsula and looked over the La Orotava Valley, he noticed how the vegetation adapted to the conditions from coastal to upper levels and thus began the science of geo-botany. The vegetation today is largely covered by banana plantations and the Valley's housing developments but **Mirador Humboldt** is still a great vantage point.

Tacoronte

At 500 metres above Tenerife's north east coast, Tacoronte has three main distinctions as far as Canarios are concerned; it's considered to have the island's best restaurants, its best wine and its worst weather. If it's cold or raining anywhere on Tenerife, it's likely to be in Tacoronte.

Constantly bustling, this historic Canarian town has more 'real' shops on its main street than there are in the whole of Playa de Las Américas and Costa Adeje. You can find just about anything you want or need in its proliferation of supermarkets, shops, furniture stores, extensive agricultural market and its bodega where they produce the award winning Viña Norte label.

Before the 20th century Tacoronte was one of the last stops on the stagecoach route for the north of Tenerife and anyone wishing to explore the island, including Alexander Von Humboldt and Richard Burton, passed through here. Today it's home to many Santa Cruz and La Laguna commuters whose large rambling houses hide behind leafy Avenidas or cluster along the slopes above the coastline.

Exploring Tacoronte's beautifully preserved old quarter, via cobbled walkways, uses just enough energy to justify lunch and a bottle of locally produced wine in one of its excellent restaurants before heading down to its coast for an afternoon on the beach – the sort of day very few British visitors ever experience.

Beaches

On the coast below the town are the settlements of El Pris and Mesa del Mar with a pleasant coastal walk linking the two.

Very much a fishing village, El Pris doesn't have any beach to speak of but has a large natural rock pool and two or three no-frills seafood restaurants.

Along the coast, boardwalks and decking provide sunbathing areas around more rock pools and a large swimming pool at Mesa del Mar. Ugly, run down, high-rise apartment blocks dominate the front and spread along the promontory looking like the desolate end of the road. But head through the tunnel to emerge onto the black sand beach of Playa de la Arena from where the concrete sprawl is hidden. No facilities or lifeguard but a café at the back of the beach and a restaurant in the campsite on the hill.

Food

There are two districts in Tacoronte that are renowned for their fine cuisine and both are located along the Carretera General del Norte.

On the La Laguna side of town is the area known as Los Naranjeros; a Valhalla for foodies where even the King of Spain dines when he visits, more specifically at **Los Limoneros** (922 63 66 37; C General Del Norte) where he's one of the few people who can afford to pay the bill.

On the El Sauzal side, restaurants line the road offering the best of Canarian and international cuisine.

By contrast, at **El Calvario** (922 56 37 34; C/El Calvario, 65) there are no rose petals on the tablecloths, come to think of it, there are no tablecloths, but the food's good, plentiful and cheap.

Accommodation

There are some nice rural houses in and around town, bookable through **ACANTUR**, the rural tourism association (*www.ecoturismocanarias.com*).

On the headland above Mesa del Mar there's a small campsite where you can stay in little wooden cabins with camp beds and the bare minimum of home comforts.

La Alhóndiga - Tacoronte

Tegueste

Tegueste is a hidden gem; not least due to the interminable road works which send drivers perpetually *away* from the town.

It's an independent municipality made up of two extremely picturesque settlements, Tegueste and El Socorro, set 200 metres above sea level in the humid Valle de Guerra which is known as Tenerife's greenhouse and is famed for its cultivation of ornamental plants.

Completely surrounded by the municipality of La Laguna, Tegueste is like an island, but without the sea, which hasn't stopped it from being obsessed with boats.

The volcanic soil and humid climate combine to produce delicious potatoes and plump, aromatic grapes which yield excellent wines.

Hell-bent on preserving its agricultural heritage and its traditions, the municipality has a thriving agricultural market; a penchant for the national sport of *Lucha Canario* and some of the most unusual and colourful fiestas of the island.

Food

With such an abundance of fresh produce, as you'd expect, even the humblest café produces fresh, traditional fare but for something really special, follow the endless dirt track that passes for the road to the Bodega El Lomo to reach the farmhouse setting of **Casa Mi Suegra** (922 63 69 02; C/ San Ignacio, 17) where rustic charm meets culinary excellence to give you the 'Tegueste' treatment.

Accommodation

Hotels, guesthouses and apartments are conspicuous by their absence but the rural tourism association (*www.ecoturismocanarias.com*) has a lovely finca for rent on the road that joins the two settlements.

Fiestas

When, in the 17th century, bubonic plague infected the entire surrounding area, Tegueste remained disease free; a 'miracle' credited to San Marcos. In thanks for his help, the town chose to build something that would require skills not hitherto held and thus, being landlocked, they built boats with billowing white sails and mounted them on wheels.

Every year on San Marcos' feast day the town holds a **Romería** in which the boats are pulled by oxen, along with carts ornately decorated with seeds and grain, the whole scene a sort of mobile work of art.

Once every three years the Teguesteros re-enact their part in keeping Santa Cruz safe from pirate attacks by staging a wonderfully colourful, night time pageant involving a full scale castle being erected in front of the Town Hall from which cannon and artillery defend the battlements against galleons. There are costumes, fireworks, animals and a very touching rendition of Ave Maria during which all the townsfolk hold aloft sparklers; trust me, you had to be there. **The Librea** is next due to be held in September 2011.

Attractions

The **Museo de Antropologia de Tenerife** (MHAT) (*www.museosdetenerife.org*) has a fascinating and beautiful collection of artefacts chronicling 500 years of traditional costumes, agriculture, ceramics, musical instruments and household objects set within the immaculately restored 18th century Casa de Carta and its extensive gardens.

One look at the neat rows of vines that carpet the hillsides tells you you're not far from a spicy white or a smoky, vanilla red.

Bodega El Lomo (*www.bodegaellomo.com*) produces wines from the Listán, Malvasia and Negromoll grapes from fresh whites to oak aged reds. Guided tours of the vines and the vaults, wine tasting and of course, the chance to buy; it'll take a steady nerve to resist blowing a week's budget in a day.

EAST TENERIFE

Arid, windy and sunny, the eastern side of the island is the least commercialised of Tenerife's coasts.

The busy TF1 motorway runs along its length from the island's capital city and port of Santa Cruz, to the southern coastal resorts of Los Cristianos and Playa de Las Américas. Around the motorway the landscape is characterised by *malpaís*; badlands of volcanic cones, pale pumice cliffs and dusty desert punctuated by industrial estates and power pylons. It's an ugly coast that for most visitors is only viewed from the window of a moving vehicle.

Motorway exits lead to the coastal towns of Candelaria and Puertito de Güímar, then to smaller settlements as the road travels further south. Outside of the vibrant, Cosmopolitan Santa Cruz and the much quieter Candelaria, there are very few concessions to tourism along this coast. Around Eras, Poris and Abades characterless housing developments are springing up behind the windswept sand dunes with the occasional pizza restaurant and small supermarket but the area feels like a desolate construction site.

In summer, the east coast beaches fill with the mobile homes of Canarios who take to the impromptu and illegal coastal campsites for their two week vacation.

Beyond the rocky shore the outline of Gran Canaria shimmers on the horizon. Inland from the motorway, the white propellers of modern windmills give testament to the near constant trade winds that sweep this coast. Running parallel above the TF1, lining the old road that first joined north and south of the island, are now-forgotten small rural settlements that still till the soil by hand and store their produce in caves while in the upper reaches virgin pine forests conceal a matrix of walking paths where you can amble all day without seeing another soul.

Anaga Mountains

Seven million years in the making, covering a huge swathe of Tenerife's north eastern tip, the Anaga Mountains are the most beautiful part of the island and also the least explored.

It's a sign of the times that what was once the most populated area of Tenerife, due to its fertile soil, is now one of the least populated; the modern settler preferring the promise of sunshine over good farming country.

The TF12 road traverses a ridge dissecting contrasting microclimates. Arid slopes descend on the eastern side towards the capital, Santa Cruz. On the northern side, ancient laurisilva forests, the likes of which have been lost to most of the rest of the world, spread with a velvet-like consistency through deep ravines. Their emerald slopes broken only by the speckled white dots of tiny hamlets tucked into in their folds and perched on rocky outcrops.

Agriculture is the mainstay of the economy as it has been since pre-conquest times. In picturesque hamlets like Afur, Chinamada (where most of the inhabitants still live in caves – albeit ones with modern facades), Taganana and La Cumbrilla (whose houses are linked by little more than goat trails), farming techniques have changed little over the centuries. The terrain is too steep for machinery, so crops are sewn, tended and harvested by hand.

The whole area is a nature lover's adventure playground and the best way to explore it is by foot along one of the many old merchant trails which were once the lifeline with the outside world. It can be cool in the mountains, so layers are essential.

Beaches

It's not only the landscape which is bare at the black sand beach of Las Gaviotas on the eastern coast; it's where the Santa Cruceros come for an all over tan. There's a café above the beach where you can have a beer in the buff.

The small beach and harbour at Roque de Bermejo lies beside the hamlet of the same name, the most remote on Tenerife. The only way to reach it is by boat, or a three hour trek from Chamorga.

Food

Pucheros (stews) and *cabra* (goat) are common in the hills (**Restaurant Cruz del Carmen**, **Casa Carlos** on the TF12 and **Casa Jose Canón** in Afur) whilst on the coast, *pescado encebollado* (fish in onion sauce) is popular, especially in the fish restaurants at Roque de las Bodegas.

Accommodation

No hotels, but rural houses are dotted around. A basic, but convenient base is the **Montes de Anaga Hostel** (922 82 20 56; *www.alberguestenerife.net*) near El Bailadero in the heart of the Anagas.

Attractions

Wherever you venture in the Anagas, you'll be assaulted by 'stop you in your tracks' scenery; the ultimate being the 360° panorama at the Pico del Ingles mirador.

Cruz del Carmen is an ideal base for long and short walks; there's a good restaurant, a visitors' centre with free walking maps (better used as 'guidelines' as they have a *mas o menos* approach to detailed directions) and a weekend farmers' market (open 10.00 -15.00 Saturday & Sunday).

The Anaga coastline viewed from Punta de Hidalgo

Arico

Located in the hills overlooking the south east coast, any route to Arico involves negotiating winding roads. Agriculture is the mainstay of the economy, predominantly potatoes and tomatoes grown in rows of neat *jable* terraces around the three towns of Villa de Arico, Arico Viejo and Arico Nuevo. Villa de Arico and

Arico Viejo are typical of the farming communities found along the old road which linked Santa Cruz with the south of the island before the TF1 autopista was built in the early 70s. In Villa de Arico, the 18th century Iglesia de San Juan Bautista with its baroque façade and Portuguese influenced bell dome towers is one of the most attractive churches on Tenerife; however neighbouring Arico Nuevo is the real surprise package in these hills. The small village is quite unique and still something of a 'secret'; you get the impression that the locals are quite happy to keep it that way. It's a sleepy hollow built by wealthy landowners in the 18th century which still exudes an air of exclusivity.

It's easy to bypass the village as the main road barely skirts its boundaries. A narrow, cobbled road descends from the small car park at the top of the village past whitewashed old houses with green windows and doorframes to a quiet, quaint little square flanked by the Iglesia de Nuestra Señora de la Luz and wonderful old buildings with lopsided roofs. Narrow paths lead from the square beyond enticing wooden gates fronting leafy courtyards overlooked by rickety balconies. The only colour on many streets, apart from white and green, is provided by the luminescent petals of bougainvillea trailing over walls. Arico Nuevo is a perfectly preserved example of rural living in a bygone age.

Food

This small, little known area produces some of the tastiest cheeses in the world and that's official. Arico's goat's cheeses, coated with paprika and gofio, have won gold medals at the World Cheese Awards. Deliciously smoky with a soft creamy texture and a hint of wild herbs, they're good enough to have Wallace and Gromit changing allegiance. Drizzled with fresh local honey, it's simply a case of love at first bite.

Restaurants around Arico are mainly simple, traditional affairs except for the stylish, **El Pimentón** (922 76 84 86; La Plaza) located in Arico Nuevo's picturesque plaza. Homely rooms with terracotta walls and soft lighting give the place a cosy atmosphere to sample local goodies from the menu accompanied by a bottle of pleasantly aromatic Flor de Chasna from Arico's bodega just along the road.

Accommodation

For a true 'far from the madding crowd' experience, book into one of Arico Nuevo's *casas rurales* like the rustic **El Sitio de la Casa** (922 76 80 21; C/La Luz, 14; *www.elsitiodelacasa.net*) which has four wonderfully atmospheric houses for rent.

Attractions

The road leading into the mountains from Villa de Arico's church ends at **La Escalada**, a deep rift in the earth with plunging walls of golden rocks accentuated by ledges, chimneys and impossible looking overhangs. It's a natural theme park for rock climbers, considered one of the best areas for crag climbing in Europe by those who know about these sorts of things.

Candelaria

Lying on the east coast 18 km below Santa Cruz in a long, thin strip that climbs back from the seafront in a charmless jungle of high-rise apartment blocks, Candelaria is Tenerife's spiritual capital.

Annually thousands of pilgrims, and daily almost as many tour buses, travel to Plaza de la Patrona where the Virgin of Candelaria, Patron Saint of the Canary Islands, is housed in a grand basilica. Lining the plaza in which it stands are nine bronze, life-sized statues of the former Guanche Menceys who ruled the island before the Spanish conquest.

In the narrow streets around the Plaza, shops provide everything the pilgrim and visitor could want from food and drink to souvenirs and religious icons. On Wednesday afternoons, Saturdays and Sundays a small market selling fresh fruit, vegetables and local produce buzzes with activity.

A pleasant promenade follows the 3 km coastline past a harbour and marina to the most northerly section of the town where its only hotels are located.

Beaches

An uninviting pebbly shoreline hems the town with an occasional small area of black sand mingling with the pebbles. In parts an attempt has been made to import golden sand but the effect is more builders' merchants than beach.

Food

Boasting more than 100 tapas dishes available in its bars, restaurants and tascas, the town has five *Rutas de Tapas* (tapas routes) available from the tourist office which you can follow, sampling small portions from various eateries at around €2/€3 each.

Accommodation

For most people, this is a day visit rather than a base for their stay so despite its size, Candelaria has only two hotels: the 4 star Catalonia Punta del Rey (922 50 18 99; Avda. Generalísimo, 165; *www.hoteles-catalonia.com*) and the 3 star Tenerife Tour (922 50 02 00; Avda. Generalísimo, 170; *www.tenerifetour.com*). Both are located at the Playa de las Caletillas end of town and are in need of a make-over.

Nightlife

The Plaza de la Patrona and the football stadium occasionally play host to international artists like Craig David and Ricky Martin.

Fiestas

The biggest religious fiesta in Tenerife's calendar is the **Virgen de Candelaria** which takes place on the 15th August to commemorate the discovery of a Gothic carving of a Black Madonna and child by two Guanche shepherds in 1390. On the eve of the fiesta, thousands of pilgrims travel by foot from all over the island, some of them ending their journey on hands and knees as they approach the basilica. The next day, a re-enactment of the 'miracle' of the Virgen's discovery is acted out in the Plaza de la Patrona.

Attractions

Climb the steps behind the basilica, cross C/La Palma and the cream building above the red tiled roof straight in front of you is **Casa las Miquelas** (922 50 52 16; C/Isla de La Gomera, 17; *www.candelaria.es*); a small pottery museum where they still throw pottery by hand. Traditionally the craft of women, the workshop shows the rudimentary tools and methods used to produce the red pots which are typical of the area. Visitors can watch the pottery being made, buy a genuine piece of Tenerife's history and help to keep this once vital craft alive.

Güímar

Once known as the 'Gateway to the South', Güímar is a town of two halves. The main commercial centre and old quarter sits at 300 metres above Tenerife's east coast on the road which formerly was the only link between the north and south of the island. On the other side of the TF1 motorway which changed all that, is Puertito, Güímar's delightful little coastal settlement.

Hogging the coastline is volcanic *malpaís*, or badlands, with a desolate outlook and plentiful indigenous plants, lizards and butterflies.

Home to the late Norwegian adventurer Thor Heyerdahl, of Kon Tiki fame, Güímar is the site of his brainchild and Tenerife's most enigmatic theme park; the Pirámides de Güímar.

Beaches

Small, black sand, pebbly coves dot the coastline around Puertito de Güímar. There are no facilities or lifeguard and to be honest, not much beach either.

Better by far are the decking and the long pier that border the harbour providing attractive sunbathing areas beside clear, turquoise waters.

Food

In town, **La Zapatería** (922 51 28 59; Calle Santo Domingo, 13) has a small but perfect tapas menu in a quaint former shoemaker's shop surrounded by a load of old cobblers, and you'll find traditional fare with Gordon Ramsey-type flair in a former tobacco drying barn in the grounds of the finca **Hotel Rural Finca Salamanca.**

At **Chibusque** (922 52 87 98; Av. Cristóbal Colón, 3A) the kitchen's set in a cave while the outside, and only, dining area overlooks the aqua waters of Puertito's harbour. The perfect spot for a long fish and seafood lunch on a sunny day.

Accommodation

Hotel Rural La Casona (922 51 02 29; C/Santo Domingo, 32; *www.hotelruraltenerife.com*) has oak floors polished to a blinding shine, low doorways to crack your skull on, beamed ceilings and an antique bed; all the joys of a beautifully restored 16th century house in the heart of town.

Just outside town you'll find the rustic charm of **Hotel Rural Finca Salamanca** (922 51 45 30; C/ Güímar; *www.hotel-fincasalamanca.com*), a converted manor house with landscaped gardens and an award-winning restaurant in the old barn.

Fiestas

Bajada de El Socorro - When two Guanche shepherds encountered a woman and her child on the beach at Socorro it changed their lives and the history of the archipelago. Every 7th September, thousands of devotees carry the statue of their Patron Saint back to where they found her and re-enact that historic day.

Attractions

The Pirámides de Güímar (*www.piramidesdeguimar.net*) – is based around the discovery of the remains of what Thor Heyerdahl believed were stepped, solar aligned pyramids like the ones in Mexico and Peru. The tranquil, enigmatic park is a showcase for Heyerdahl's evidence to support the theory that ancient peoples could have sailed the Atlantic in reed boats long before Columbus laid claim to being the first to do so.

A museum, film show and replicas of Heyerdahl's reed ships all add interest to the pyramids themselves and make up one of Tenerife's most enduring mysteries.

Avoid Thursdays when the tour groups go.

San Andrés

The white houses of the little fishing village of San Andrés tumble down the Anaga Mountains to the edge of the sea on the north east tip of Tenerife.

Just around the headland is the frenetic capital city, but it might as well be a hundred kilometres away for all the impact it has on San Andrés.

Characterised by its precipitous setting and the 'Broken Tower' of Torre de San Andrés which lies in pieces at its feet, the village has had more titles than a book shop. Throughout the 16th and 17th centuries it was known as 'the pirate port' because it was subject to constant incursions from corsairs.

Water rich from its position at the confluence of two barrancos, the village produced so much fruit and vegetables for Santa Cruz that it was known as 'the city's larder'. Today it's known as 'the gateway to the Anagas'.

But wander its streets anytime after 1pm and the all pervading aroma of fresh fish grilling on open coals will tell you that it's also known for its fish restaurants and is a lunch time favourite with Santacruceros.

Beaches

The tropical paradise of Las Teresitas may have been constructed for the citizens of Santa Cruz but it's on San Andrés doorstep (quite literally, as the east coast breeze carries the fine sand), lending every villager a picture postcard vista from their front terrace.

Framed by the stunning backdrop of the Anaga Mountains and backed by rows of lush palms swaying in the breeze, the white sand beach is the archetypal tropical paradise.

Clear, turquoise waters are tamed by a man made breakwater and provide a haven for tropical fish and a freeform swimming pool for the beach, which at 1.5 kilometres in length, can swallow half the city without even looking busy.

There are kiosks, toilets, showers and changing rooms along the back of the beach and loads of parking spaces.

Las Teresitas beach below San Andrés

Food

The ratio of restaurants to residents in San Andrés is testament to its popularity as a venue to travel to for lunch.

At **Rincon de Pescadores** (922 59 10 44; corner of C/ Chana Cabrera) you'll know what's on the menu at the

110

same time as the owner; it's whatever's in the fisherman's basket when he knocks on the side door mid morning.

If you don't mind the company of hungry fishermen, head for the no-frills **Los Pinchitos** (922 54 92 83; Calle Guillén, 14) where the fish is cooked simply, and is simply delicious.

About as avante-garde as San Andrés gets, **La Posada Del Pez** (922 54 95 36; Carretera de Taganana, 2) has a more contemporary look, both to its décor and its menu.

Accommodation

It's rumoured that plans are afoot to build a hotel behind Las Teresitas, but for the moment only rural houses offer a place to lay your head. The rural tourism agency Viajes AECAN (922 24 81 14; *www.aecan.com*) has a couple of nice places to rent in the village.

Nightlife

Everyone either goes fishing or to Santa Cruz.

Santa Cruz

"Probably many people have shared my feeling of disappointment on landing at Santa Cruz... but even so, the utter hideousness of the capital of Teneriffe was a shock to me."
Florence Du Kane, "The Canary Islands" published 1911

Not the most auspicious of introductions to the island's capital city it has to be said, and one which until recently, it was difficult to argue with. But with the 21st Century has come a vast, and vastly overdue, facelift for Santa Cruz.

Today, the millions of people who annually arrive at the port in the world's ocean liners are greeted by the white iconic tsunami of Calatrava's Auditorium, César

Manrique's Parque Marítimo and Plaza España's strikingly eclectic blend of Franco symbolism and urban modernism.

Although the sprawling ugliness of the CEPSA oil refinery remains a blot on the south side of the city, a great deal has been done in the last five years to bring Santa Cruz into focus as a potential tourist destination. Not least, the addition of a sleek and sexy tram system and the development of the Noria District which is burgeoning with contemporary bars and chic restaurants. Further plans are afoot to pedestrianise the portside and create a green walkway lined with shops, cafes and cinemas to add to the already substantial choice of first class shopping in the city.

Spreading south from the foot of the dramatic Anaga Mountains on the north east coast of Tenerife, the settlement of Santa Cruz got its name in 1494 when Fernández de Lugo arrived to begin his assault on the island. To celebrate his safe landing, de Lugo placed a cross in the ground around which a mass was held and the place became known as Santa Cruz, or Holy Cross.

When, in 1706 the port of Garachico was destroyed by a volcanic eruption, Santa Cruz took up the mantel of the island's premier port and a booming trade at the crossroads to the New World brought expansion and riches.

With wealth came further attempted incursions, most notably by Admiral Nelson who in 1797 led an attack on Santa Cruz in which he lost over 150 men, his right arm and the battle.

Generous in victory, General Gutiérrez sent Nelson a barrel of the island's finest Malmsey wine. Nelson reciprocated with a barrel of ale and a cheese; an imbalance of cultural exchange between Britain and Tenerife which has remained a custom to this day.

Beaches

If you plan to create an extensive, golden beach where currently only a small, black sand and pebble cove exists, it helps to have a handy supply of raw materials. Thus in 1973, four million sacks of Spanish Sahara were deposited 8 km outside Santa Cruz to create the fine, white sand paradise of **Las Teresitas.**

Palm tree lined, with adequate parking for half the city, a stone breakwater keeps out the wild Atlantic rollers and creates a tranquil bay perfect for swimming and snorkelling.

Kiosks are dotted along the rear of the beach serving tapas, snacks and cold beers or you can sample some of the best fish restaurants on the island in the quaint fishing village of San Andrés which climbs the hillside like a refugee from a Greek island.

Alongside the parking area there are showers, changing booths and toilets whose locking mechanism takes the skills of a safe-cracker to decipher.

Food

As befits any capital city, you'll find an endless choice of places to eat from intimate tascas like **Bodeguita Canarias** (922 29 32 16) on Calle Imeldo Seris or **Tasca de Enfrente** (922 27 10 97) alongside Parque García to top drawer restaurants like **El Coto de Antonio** (922 27 21 05) on Calle General Goded or **Los Menceys** (922 60 99 00) in the Sheraton Mencey Hotel. Cuisine is international with the usual emphasis on traditional Canarian and Basque dishes.

For a more bohemian setting with a choice of menus that include contemporary touches, try **Los Reunidos** (922 24 10 28) or **Mojo y Mojitos** (922 28 16 41) in the Noria District.

Accommodation

Rub shoulders with the rich and famous or at least, the few rich and famous who ever stay on Tenerife, in the city's only 5 star hotel, **The Sheraton Mencey** (922 60 99 00; C/ Dr Jose Naveiras, 38; *www.sheraton.com/mencey*). Grandeur on the scale of Versailles, the hotel even has its own casino; you could lose your head over it, or at very least your shirt.

Trade luxury for convenience and a prime location with the 3 star **Stil Plaza Hotel** (922 27 24 53; Plaza Candelaria, 10; *www.hotelplazastil.com*). No frills city centre hotel.

Style gurus will feel comfortable in the 3 star **Hotel Taburiente** (922 27 60 00; C/ Dr Jose Naveiras, 24A; *www.hoteltaburiente.com*) alongside the Parque García; contemporary and minimalist with the emphasis on chic.

Nightlife

Head into the Noria District which runs from the foot of the landmark grey stone tower of the Iglesia de La Concepción to find many of the city's newest and coolest bars where live bands feature on summer weekends and you can drink until 2 or 3am.

After that, head over to the area around Parque Marítimo near the auditorium for the clubs.

Watch local press and the free 'Agenda' booklet for live gigs and events such as Santa Blues.

Fiestas

Carnaval – There really ought to be loud music and tickertape at the very mention of the word. Europe's largest and second only to Rio in world terms, Santa Cruz Carnaval is *the* highlight of the year.

Carnaval Queen

Originating from the practice of using up all the sinful meat and dairy produce before Catholics entered the abstinence of Lent, it's now an excuse for one almighty blow out in which party stamina and endurance are tested beyond the limits.

Characterised by parades at the beginning and end of the main week in which hundreds of costumed revellers, scantly clad dancers and flamboyantly

115

decorated floats thread their way through the heart of the city, the real spirit of Carnaval is in the nightly street parties held in Plaza España and attended by hundreds of thousands of people.

To really enjoy Carnaval, go native and get into fancy dress for the nightly parties (many people have a different costume for every night) and don't bother arriving at the Plaza much before midnight. A couple of things worth thinking about when you choose your costume are firstly February nights can be chilly and secondly you're going to be on your feet for a very long time; hence the popularity of animal jumpsuits and trainers.

Attractions

Sculpture Trail - Slip on the comfy shoes and start out from La Rambla to discover a cornucopia of eclectic sculptures, most of them the legacy of an exhibition in 1974, by such luminaries as Joan Miró and Henry Moore. The route will take you into the city's oasis of **Parque García Sanabria** to see the voluptuous 'Fertility' in her fountain and then back to port side for the 'Angel of Victory' and more. Pick up a guide at the tourist office or go on one of their tours.

Museum of Man and Nature (MNH) (922 20 93 20; Calle Fuente Morales; *www.museosdetenerife.org)* is housed in the splendid 19th century, Neoclassical former hospital for the homeless. Three floors of exhibitions take you from the explosive birth of the Canary Islands through their climate and bio-diversity to the mummified remains of their first known inhabitants, the Guanche.

PRIDE, PASSION, LOYALTY
WITH CD TENERIFE & ARMADA SUR

It's another scorching day and of course I am wearing shorts, the football shirt is unfamiliar, but worn with pride, but what really attracts strange looks from bare skinned holiday makers is my woolly football scarf. Don't worry, it's not sunstroke, just another affliction, I'm a fan of CD Tenerife (*www.clubdeportivotenerife.es*)

They may not be my first love but they have become a much loved mistress, and the atmosphere of a live Spanish league game is a unique experience. Half of the fun of going to a game is the comradeship of shared despair or elation and for that you couldn't ask for better company than the Armada Sur (*www.armadasur.com*)

The name means South Army and if that conjures up unwelcome images of marauding hooligans, rest assured that the only battling this army does is to get pole position at the bar. CD Tenerife play in the Segunda Division, just one below Real Madrid, Barcelona etc, and attract 10,000 plus fans to home games in Santa Cruz. In 1989 Chris Todd "The General" moved over from Aldershot, and missing his home town team and Arsenal, he looked to CDT to fill the void, and now runs this officially recognized fan club.

Home is The Toby Jug in San Eugenio Alto, where a wide range of allegiances are on display with shirts from Bolton to Brazil soon being swapped for the blanquiazul (white and blue) of Tenerife. Huge banners are unfurled and large quantities of singing juice are downed as the coach load, two for big games, assembles.

Pick up points are attended to en route with new passengers greeted with good natured abuse about their "home" teams but with a whole hour to Santa Cruz a refueling stop is essential at the Oasis restaurant bar half way up the motorway. The ground is normally reached an hour before the game allowing a relaxing top up in the local bar while tickets are distributed.

The stadium may look dowdy and unimpressive from outside but once in, you are consumed in a swirling mass of colour and noise. All the officially recognized fan clubs or "peñas" are grouped together at the Grada popular end of the ground amid a sea of drums, flags and paper confetti and the songs and chants are constant regardless of score, weather or league position. Sorry, you wont find your half time Bovril or curled sandwiches here but full marks to the souvenir stalls for shifting hundreds of woolly scarves while the thermometer nudges the 30 degree mark.

Though mainly Brits, Armada Sur welcome all nationalities and are well accepted by the locals, mixing socially with their Canarian terrace comrades. Remember when football was fun? It still is in Tenerife, and you can even have an ice cream at half time.

Colin Kirby, freelance writer, *www.colinkirby.com*

SOUTH TENERIFE

The first views of Tenerife experienced by the millions of people who fly into Reina Sofia Airport in the south will cause scenery lovers' hearts to plummet. A hot, dry, lifeless, pumice terrain where rain is an infrequent visitor accompanies coaches along the TF1 autopista on their journey from the airport to the southern resorts.

But once you get away from the construction site landscape of the autopista, there's beauty to be found. Beaches are lapped by turquoise waters. Wind erosion has created surreal rock formations. The Adeje Mountains add drama to the skyline and the countryside between the coast and hills is pockmarked by volcanic cones.

Much of the coast is characterised by purpose built modern resorts with immaculate man made beaches. The biggest, Playa de Las Américas and Costa Adeje cater for people who want sunshine and amenities more than culture and tradition, whilst others like Los Cristianos and El Médano retain their fishing village roots and still, in the main, feel Canarian.

A popular criticism of the south of Tenerife is that it has been over developed and therefore spoiled. It's a romantic, but ill informed view.

"It's full of drunken English,
Romanians and Mafia."
Loly, a musician in a small hill town in the
north commenting on the south of Tenerife

Prior to the advent of mass tourism, there were only a few tiny fishing communities along the south coast. Most of the area was *malpaís* (arid badlands), which were of little or no use to neither man nor beast. Their transformation into a year round, sun kissed playground for northern Europeans provided a much needed boost to the island's economy.

Ultimately, anyone seeking the authentic southern Tenerife can still find it...where it always existed; in the original centres of population in the hills, in towns like Granadilla and Vilaflor where tradition and culture remain strong and life at the edge of the pine forest continues much as it always has done.

RETIRING TO TENERIFE

I have always felt the pull of foreign lands. Every holiday we went on I would longingly look in the estate agents windows and dream of living in the sun, but until my family were settled with families of their own these were only pipe dreams.

I first seriously entertained the notion of retiring abroad in the early 1990s but my husband loved his job and it was not until 10 years later he came home and completely out of the blue said, 'start looking for a new life'. After drawing up a shortlist which included being able to survive only speaking English I proceeded to dismiss Canada and Australia as being too far away from family, the climate in Cyprus too extreme.

We had never been to Tenerife, having always assumed, like many, that it was full of lager louts and loud music. However desperate for some sun we came over for a winter break and both thought what a beautiful place. Tenerife was so totally different from our general perception. We immediately fell in love with the island's diversity. We wondered what it would be like to retire here.

On returning to the UK we finally took the plunge and I went online and contacted several estate agents in the Playa de las Americas area. The agent we settled on made the whole process so easy I find it hard to believe when I read of the horrors some people go through. On a flying visit to look at suitable areas to settle in we found our ideal house (only the second we had viewed) and not wanting to lose out this forced us into bringing our plans forward by 12 months.

It didn't feel right keeping a bolt hole for when the inevitable homesickness struck, I had wanted this for so long it had to be total commitment or nothing so I left work and spent a couple of months selling our assets in England. Our home was sold at the asking price to the first people who viewed it, all of our belongings went on eBay and we made a handsome profit. I'm a great believer in Karma and it seemed that the fates were looking favourably on us – we had made the right decision. We have been here for a few years now and don't regret the decision. We love the weather - the seasons change, a winter's day here can be as warm as a summer's day in England. Our life is quite laid back; nothing is done in a rush. We made more friends in a few months than we did in a lifetime in England. Perhaps the climate makes people friendlier.

While we miss my family, we do travel to see them a couple of times a year. They also come out to Tenerife regularly. We are after all, only 4 hours away from the UK. Tenerife has added a good 10 years to my life, I'm fitter, happier and healthier than I have ever been - would I return to the UK permanently, No Way.

Aguilas, TripAdvisor destination expert
for Tenerife, www.tripadvisor.com

Costa Adeje

Costa Adeje, the glittering star in Tenerife's tourist heaven, has been the cause of a renaissance in terms of how the south is viewed as a tourist destination. A spate of luxury hotels, each with their own distinctive architectural style, has transformed the barren coastline at the western end of what was known until recently as Playa de Las Américas. Now the area is invariably referred to as the 'upmarket' resort of Costa Adeje.

The name has become an umbrella term for the area incorporating Playa del Duque, Fañabe, Torviscas, Puerto Colón and San Eugenio; all popular havens for sun seekers and many, from ordinary Joes to TV soap stars, have purchased their own little place in the sun there.

Costa Adeje has everything that anyone looking for a beach resort could want. Golden sands; ultra modern shopping centres; fashionable bars and stylish restaurants; a golf course with colonial styled clubhouse (*www.golfcostaadeje.com*) and a marina at Puerto Colón where visitors can charter yachts, go whale watching and even explore Adeje's undersea vistas from the safety of a BOB (an undersea scooter - *www.bob-diving.com*). What it lacks, like most purpose built resorts, is the soul which exists in Tenerife's original towns.

For that you need to travel inland a short distance to Adeje town, nestling below the mountain range of the same name. The town, a favourite haunt for Sir Francis Drake, who had dubious business dealings in the area, lies at the opposite end of the spectrum from its coastal cousin. Here cobblers and tile makers still toil away inside dim doorways on pleasant tree lined streets leading to the town centre and the 16th century Iglesia de Santa Úrsula. It's a location which should appeal to anyone wanting to experience authentic Canarian living within a stone's throw of the sort of facilities which attract millions of visitors annually.

> *"I came out of the hotel one day and turned left (toward San Eugenio) instead of right (toward Playa del Duque). OH MY GOD, it was awful!"*
> Linda, a tourist staying in Costa Adeje for the first time

On Costa Adeje's western perimeter, the small fishing village of La Caleta hasn't quite been engulfed by the plush developments inching towards it and for the moment retains the air of a sleepy fishing community.

Beaches

Costa Adeje boasts a number of attractive, man made golden beaches; all spotlessly clean with lifeguards, sunbeds and toilet facilities. They're protected by breakwaters, making swimming a leisurely and relatively current free experience.

Playa del Duque seems the most exclusive, probably because it fronts swish hotels and views to the main tourist developments in the south are blocked by a volcanic outcrop. Turquoise seas, thatched umbrellas and striped huts give the beach a Caribbean meets St Tropez appearance.

The sweeping beaches of Playa Fañabe and Playa Torviscas merge into one another; there's an inflatable green iceberg in the centre of the bay for water babies of all ages to practice their penguin impersonations.

Choose Playa del Bobo in San Eugenio for windsurfing and sailing lessons. Next door are Playas de Troya I and II which have a whole range of activities from parasailing and jet skis to diving.

It's still possible to get away from the crowds without having to travel too far. Trek across the headland at La Caleta and you'll be rewarded with some secluded coves inhabited by only the odd hippy or two.

Food

Adeje is known for its garlic chicken dishes. They're highly addictive and once tried, bound to become a favourite. The best restaurants to sample some are in Adeje town. **Oasis** (922 78 08 23; C/ Grande) probably serves the tastiest. It's unpretentious and good value.

La Vieja (922 71 15 48; Avda Las Gaviotas) in La Caleta mixes good cooking with stylish décor. The menu includes classic Spanish seafood dishes like Basque favourite *bacalao al pil-pil* as well as a selection of Canarian fish. Add a good wine list and a view of the sunset over La Gomera and you've got a winning combination.

El Molino Blanco (922 79 62 82; Avda Austria, 5) is set in gardens where diners sit beneath a full sized windmill (whose sails are lit up at night) and are serenaded by a singing chef. So over the top kitsch, it's great. The mainly traditional menu is good too.

A romantic spot for dinner is the terrace of **Las Rocas** (922 74 60 00; C/Gran Bretaña) which juts out over the ocean giving it a secluded air. Opt for a seafood dish when the sunset bathes the terrace in a golden glow and you're asking for an aphrodisiac overdose; although the ardour might be doused when the bill arrives.

Accommodation

With 5 star accommodations galore, luxury seekers are spoilt for choice. **La Plantación del Sur** (922 71 77 73; C/Roque Nublo, 1; *www.vinccihoteles.com*) is voguishly stylish and a more adult and sophisticated 5 star than many of its 'theme park' neighbours. Located slightly back from the coast, this is dark chocolate as compared to milk.

The Hotel Jardín Tropical (902 25 02 51; C/Gran Bretaña; *www.jardin-tropical.com*) is a good mid-range choice. Located within easy access of both the main areas of Costa Adeje and Playa de Las Américas, it has an attractive Moorish design and the lush subtropical gardens are popular with guests looking for quiet corners to lose themselves in a good book. Ask for a room with seaview.

Travellers with a taste for the authentic Tenerife will prefer the 200 year old coach house, **Hotel El Fondo** (922 78 15 50; C/Grande, 26) in the centre of Adeje old town. Eleven en suite rooms are centred around a courtyard; there's also an atmospheric restaurant whose tables and chairs spill out onto the character filled streets.

Nightlife

The main hub of bars and clubs are located in the San Eugenio area; these are aimed at people who want familiar environments and on tap entertainment when they go abroad; any number of interchangeable Irish, Scottish, English, karaoke and sports bars are the order of the day.

Costa Adeje's renaissance has seen a few international style bars creep onto the nocturnal scene, some of these like the Moorish **Acantur** and the **Amber Lounge** are located around the more select del Duque area, whilst others; the **Faro Chill Out** bar (Puerto Colón) and **Monkey Beach Bar** (on the border with Las Américas) are more scattered. A criticism often levelled at the Playa del Duque area is that there isn't a great choice of nightlife.

Fiestas

Adeje town comes over all 'luvvy' on Good Friday, when many of the townspeople take a role in a full blown re-enactment of the Passion of Christ that would rival Mel Gibson's version; it's surprisingly evocative.

Attractions

The newest 'WOW' attraction in town is the Thai themed **Siam Park** (*www.siampark.net*). A beautifully landscaped water park with imaginative white knuckle rides (the Tower of Power is only for the bravest, or foolhardy) set amidst rich tropical gardens. Built by the owners of Loro Parque and displaying the same commitment to quality, it's a little bit of Thailand in Tenerife.

Aqualand (*www.aqualand.es*) another water park with a dolphin show is located next door to **Siam Park**. However whether it can successfully compete with its attractive new neighbour is a much debated question.

The most popular walk in Tenerife is **Barranco del Infierno** at the edge of Adeje town. A one and a half hour trek through a ravine ends at a small waterfall. It's pleasant enough, but there are better walks on Tenerife where enjoying nature doesn't cost you anything (you have to pay for this one). Entrance is limited, so book in advance (922 78 28 85).

El Médano

In everything but the weather, El Médano is Tenerife's coolest resort.

Seldom absent easterly winds attract local and international kiteboarders and wind surfers who spend their days in hand to sail combat with the elements, skimming the ocean alongside three kilometres of natural golden sands.

The same winds keep the serious suntan seekers of the more popular southern resorts at bay leaving El Médano to a laid back, stylish, Bohemian clientele who take their sunshine with a healthy helping of local culture.

Grown from a small fishing village, El Médano has retained its Canarian population and swelled their numbers with sports-minded incomers who have opened surf schools, surf bars and surf shops along the wooden 'paseo' that lines the seafront.

Plaza de Asturias, which is the focal point of the village, is busy with its pavement cafes, doubling as the venue for a weekend market where neo-hippies lay out their clothing, jewellery and craft stalls, and as the open air stage for World Music concerts and the occasional theatre production.

The landmark red volcanic cone of Montaña Roja lies to the west of the resort, acting as a stunning backdrop to the gold sand and petrol waters of this vibrant, photogenic part of Tenerife's southern coast.

Provided you suit the 'windswept and interesting' look, El Médano represents the perfect blend of a coastal resort with long, golden sand beaches, near-guaranteed all year round sunshine and some genuine Tinerfeñan culture; there aren't many places on the island that can boast the same.

Beaches

If beaches were currency, El Médano would be the Sir Paul McCartney of Tenerife. No less than seven sandy sites grace the resort from Playa de la Pelada in the east to Playa La Tejita in the west.

Many of the natural golden sand beaches are given over to El Médano's first two loves; surfing and naturism.

One of the seven sandy beaches of El Médano

Surfers have the whole of the beautiful Playa Machado to themselves and its fine sand is constantly littered with their boards and sails. At the headland on the east of the village is Playa El Cabezo which hosts international windsurfing competitions and further along to the east is Playa La Jaquita which also fills the horizon with sails.

Those who prefer to have no 'white bits' head out to Playa La Pelada and scramble down the rocks to the resort's main nudist spot where the sheltered coves

127

keep out the wind and the 'sightseers'. Around the base of Bocinegro to the west is the small beach of La Playita which is popular with male naturists and the cove at the foot of Montaña Roja on Playa La Tejita is also given over to nude sunbathing.

If neither surfing nor nudism ring your bell, the town beach of Playa El Médano has fine sand and a gently shelving shoreline and is very popular with families. Backed by bars, restaurants, ice cream parlours and kiosks, you'll want for nothing all day.

For that Bounty advert feeling, walk for 20 minutes towards Montaña Roja, past the sand dunes and through the *malpaís* until you arrive at the white sand paradise of Playa La Tejita which could absorb coach loads of visitors but luckily, doesn't. Just past the nudists' cove, a straw roofed beach bar dispenses cold beers and cool sounds while you wander the turquoise shore leaving virgin footprints in the sand.

Food

El Médano's culinary offerings are as diverse as its visitors and you'll find Canarian, Mexican and even a Japanese sushi bar amongst its eclectic collection.

As you'd expect for such a Bohemian venue, there are plenty of veggie offers on menus and even vegans will find themselves at home in the **Jungle Lounge Bar** (922 17 98 95; C/José Bello) which uses tofu and seitan to great effect in its dishes.

Try some of the best tapas in the south at **El Timón** (922 17 66 01) and **Playa Chica** (922 17 72 94) on Paseo Marcial García where tables are squeezed onto small terraces and on the beach front in these ever popular establishments.

Push the gastronomic boat out with a visit to **Yaiza** (922 17 89 52; C/Iriarte, 12) whose bland exterior belies the sumptuous flavour of his lamb fillets and his veal stew with monkfish (sorry, veggies!).

Accommodation

There are a proliferation of apartments in and around the town, from cheap bedsits to swish apartments overlooking Playa Machado; **Holiday Rentals UK** has as good a selection as anyone else (*www.holiday-rentals.co.uk*)

The 3 star **Hotel El Médano** *(922 17 70 00*; Picacho, 2; *www.hotelmedano.com)* is located right in the centre of the village at the foot of Plaza Asturias and next to the town beach. Built in the 1960s, it won't win any prizes for style but it still packs some character and its sunbathing terrace on stilts over the sea is a great way to avoid getting sand in your face on characteristically breezy days.

Remarkably reasonably priced is the brand new 4 star **Hotel Arenas Del Mar** *(922 17 98 30*; Avda Europa, 2; *www.hotelarenasdelmar.com)* behind Playa La Jaquita; it's a real touch of class. Try it before they wise up and add a nought to the price.

Nightlife

After a hard day on the boards, the order of the night is laid back and mellow. Indulge in an early cava with the surf dudes at **Flashpoint**, on the boardwalk behind Playa Machado, before heading over the other side of town to Plaza Roja where you can kick back at **Manfred's Soul Café** and enjoy the sunset chill-out or join in the jam sessions.

Attractions

This is the wind surfing and kiteboarding capital of Tenerife; if it's got anything to do with riding waves, you can hire it, learn it, wear it and buy it here. With up to 290 days of wind a year and sea temperatures that hover around the high 60°s, you can surf your way through the calendar. Equipment hire is around €35 per day and lessons start from around €30 a session including equipment (*www.kitecenter-medano.com*; *www.surfcenter.el-medano.com*).

Granadilla de Abona

Granadilla de Abona nestles into the hillside at around the 600 metre mark, where the buff *jable* (pumice) landscape meets the edge of the pine forest. Its location makes it suitable for visitors interested in rural living and outdoor pursuits such as walking, rock climbing and mountain biking.

There's a pleasantly nostalgic feel to Granadilla's streets. Shops are reminiscent of the kind of independent affairs found in British towns in the 1960s, with shoe and shirt boxes piled high behind wooden counters and shelves full of all sorts of household goods. The butchers, fishmonger and greengrocer are all located in the same courtyard with a bar and takeaway tapas bar (fast food – Granadilla style) thrown in for good measure. It has a friendly, bustling air; close enough to the tourist resorts to be convenient for commuting, but having more in common with the other agricultural communities dotted along the old Carretera General del Sur.

Some pavements on the main street are ridiculously narrow, forcing pedestrians onto the road and into the path of oncoming 4x4s. Better to stick to the mainly traffic free and more picturesque streets around the Convent San Luis (once a military headquarters complete with dungeon, now the town's library and tranquil courtyard) and the 17th century Iglesia de San Antonio de Padua whose midget gem shaped tower has a Russian Orthodox quality to it.

Food

Finding a restaurant serving good traditional local cuisine is never a problem in Tenerife's hill towns; there are plenty dotted around Granadilla serving the usual Canarian staple of grilled meats and fish dishes. But variety is the spice of life and all that, so for something different try **Casa Tagoro** (922 77 22 40; C/Tagoro, 28; *www.casatagoro.de*). To say the menu is eclectic is a bit of an understatement. There's Bavarian roast pork with dumplings, tapas, Thai, game (winter only) and even kangaroo. It's all artistically presented and the setting, around a roaring fire in the courtyard of a 200 year old mansion, is just the icing on the cake.

Accommodation

Although there are only a couple of places to rest weary heads, they're in wonderfully atmospheric buildings on two of the prettiest streets in the south of Tenerife. **Hotel Rural Senderos de Abona** (922 77 02 00; C/Peatonal Iglesia; *www.senderosdeabona.com*) is an enchanting, rustic house with courtyards and polished wooden floors which also has a restaurant and tourist information office. **El Traspatio** (922 63 05 96; C/Arquitecto Marrero. 9; *www.casaruraleltraspatio.com*) also has oodles of 'olde worlde' charm and, as the building houses three apartments, the freedom that comes with self-catering.

Attractions

The town's **History Museum** (C/Arquitecto Marrero; 11) is tiny, but beautifully designed with interesting exhibits about rural living in the south of Tenerife pre-tourism (information in Spanish only). One darkened room reveals a couple of grotesque looking mummified Guanche and scattered human bones. It's delightfully macabre.

Granadilla's a perfect base for heading into the hills to seek out the **'Paisajes Lunar'**; a series of surreal, otherworldly peaked rock formations. The lunar landscape features regularly on postcards, but most visitors have never seen them first hand.

Granadilla de Abona

Las Galletas, Costa Del Silencio & Golf Del Sur

Working eastwards from the southern tip of the island, Las Galletas is the least commercialised of the three resorts that hug this stretch of coast. Its history as a fishing village pre-dates the Spanish conquest and it still retains a large Canarian population and commensurate culture.

The focus of the village is a pretty marina in front of which the daily catch is sold from stalls and then grilled or fried and served up for lunch in the restaurants that line the promenade.

Southwards from the marina is a tranquil beach which follows the coast around to the *malpais*, or badlands that characterise the area; eight kilometres of arid desert populated by an abundance of Tenerife's endemic flora and the occasional 'bender' constructed of straw and old surf boards where the heat-hardiest of hippies hangs out.

Life in Las Galletas has a mellow pace, which is closely guarded by the locals who have no desire to mirror their neighbours to the east, or to the west of the island; evidenced by the absence of any hotels or holiday apartments in the village. And if you're looking for excitement here, think rubber...the waters that surround the resort provide Tenerife's most spectacular dive sites.

Marking the 'join' with the resort of Costa Del Silencio, are the concrete boxes and militarily ordered sunbeds of the Ten-Bel resort where, were it not for the constant sunshine, they could have recorded Hi-de-Hi.

Built in the 1960s with Belgian money, Ten-Bel was the island's first purpose built holiday complex and, save for the occasional lick of paint, little about it has changed since. The area which grew up around it and shares its complete lack of charm is known as Costa Del Silencio,

133

the name of which pre-dates the existence of the south airport and the constant drone of cement mixers and today is more of an ironic statement than a description.

Bereft of any redeeming features, row upon row of near-identical holiday, residential and retirement apartments sit in complexes alongside commercial centres filled with estate agents, souvenir shops, supermarkets and restaurants who offer bland menus to mainly Brits, Germans and Belgians.

Move further along the coast and some of the concrete is replaced by green, or rather greens, as the eponymous courses of Golf Del Sur undulate in the heat haze. Overwhelmingly British in both its population and its visitors, Golf Del Sur's hotels, shopping arcades, restaurants and bars are predominantly geared towards satisfying their needs. Rows of blackboards announce sports TV coverage, cabaret, karaoke and burger and chips.

A shiny, brand new marina, San Miguel, is already filled with yachts and cruisers even though, save for the greens that sweep down the headland and a small kiosk, there's nothing else there. Half a dozen or so cranes on the horizon add testament to the fact that Golf Del Sur is still 'under construction'.

Beaches

Las Galletas has a pleasant, sheltered sand and pebble beach from where you can watch the boats bobbing on the sun kissed waters of the marina. There are no facilities or lifeguard but you're only a stroll away from the promenade's restaurants and ice cream parlours.

Other than that, the coast around this part of Tenerife is sheer, rocky and for the most part devoid of beaches. A pleasant coastal path leads from Las Galletas to the Ten-Bel resort and it has the occasional crumbling steps down to churning rock pools for those who like their daily dip to have that frisson of danger attached.

Pretty marina at Las Galletas

Food

Fresh fish and seafood are the signature dishes of the restaurants along Las Galletas' promenade where the presence of French and Belgian visitors to this part of Tenerife adds a certain '*je ne sais quoi*' to the menus, including 'moules y frites' at the **Panorama** (922 73 01 52; Paseo Marítimo, 19).

Amongst the proliferation of Sunday Roast and Indian Takeaways that characterise Gold Del Sur is the pretty wine bar of **Dabda** (922 73 83 69; Av. José Miguel Galván Bello) where good wines and tapas can be followed by tempters like blueberry cheesecake.

But the real Rick Stein in this fleet of Harry Ramsdens is the neighbouring fishing village of **Los Abrigos** where a dozen or more fish restaurants frame a picturesque harbour. If it's snob value and Master Chef presentation you're after, **Los Roques** (922 74 94 01; C/La Marina, 16; *www.restaurantelosroques.com*) will provide it by the plate and glass full but your wallet will be considerably lighter on the way home.

Travel further into the harbour and any one of the simpler establishments will serve you up fish just as tasty but at a fraction of the price.

Accommodation

You don't have to play golf to stay in Gold Del Sur but if you do, green fees come as part of the package. The stylish 4 star **Hotel Vincci Tenerife Golf** (922 71 73 37; *www.vinccitenerifegolfhotel.com*), the contemporary 4 star **Golf Plaza Spa Resort** (922 73 70 00; *www.golfplazaresort.com*) and the peaceful 4 star **Aguamarina Golf** (922 73 89 99; Avda del Atlántico, 2; *www.gemahoteles.com*) all come up to par.

For those on a budget who don't mind using boulders to tighten guy ropes as the ground's too hard for pegs, should head to the **Nauta Campsite** (922 78 51 18; *www.campingnauta.com*) on the TF653 between Las Galletas and Guaza and pitch a tent or rent a wooden cabin. It's not cheap as campsites go (€17.60 per day for 2 people, a tent and a car) but it has every facility you can think of and a touch of that Butlins atmosphere.

Nightlife

If it's a full moon, head to the Robinson Crusoe surroundings of **Vai Moana Chill Out Bar** on the *malpaís* side of the beach in Las Galletas for their regular Full Moon party. Any other night of the week you can chill to the point of comatose in their hammocks where cocktails and the cool vibes of live Jazz, Blues, Reggae and Soul offer a sweeter alternative to the karaoke and cabaret bars of the commercial centres of Costa Del Silencio and Golf Del Sur.

Attractions

Diving – The seas around Las Galletas are deep, calm and clear, offering the perfect diving conditions for exploring rusting wrecks and volcanic rock formations teeming with life. There are dive clubs aplenty, amongst them Dive Tenerife (922 78 59 10; *www.divetenerife.com*) and Tenerife Scuba (922 78 55 84; *www.tenerifescuba.com*)

Submarine Safari (922 73 66 29; *www.submarinesafaris.com*; €48 adults, €28 children) – Leaving from the new Marina of San Miguel in Golf Del Sur this popular submarine trip takes you into the awesome underworld of Las Galletas without the aid of an oxygen tank and flippers. Packed with 'wow' moments, you'll have a memory stick full of eels, wrecks and rays and if you're old enough, 'Yellow Submarine' going round your head for days afterwards.

Golf – The Golf Del Sur course (*www.golfdelsur.net*) (27 holes, par 72) and the Amarilla Golf course (*www.amarillagolf.es*) (18 holes, par 72) have greens sweeping down to the sea and an easterly breeze to notch up the difficulty factor.

Los Cristianos

In 1957 a Swedish vet, broadcaster and MS sufferer named Bengt Rylander arrived on the south coast of Tenerife in the tiny fishing village of Los Cristianos and found that the warm, dry climate sent his condition into remission. He broadcast his discovery to the Swedish medical authorities and to his fellow MS sufferers and thus began the development of Los Cristianos as a rehabilitation centre and ultimately, mass tourism destination.

Despite its breakneck expansion, the resort still has fishing and the sea at its heart and retains a Tinerfeñan character which separates it from its purpose built neighbour.

Gateway to the Western Canary Islands of La Gomera, La Palma and El Hierro, Los Cristianos is characterised by its bustling, colourful port, one of Spain's busiest.

Narrow streets lined with shops, bars, restaurants, ice cream parlours and souvenir outlets criss-cross their way back from a wide promenade and golden beaches. On the hills behind the centre, complex after complex of holiday and residential apartments climb towards the motorway and construction cranes are an ever present feature of the horizon.

Home to a large British ex-pat population and preferred destination of retired Brit 'swallows' who over-winter on its sunny beaches, Los Cristianos is considerably quieter than its rowdy neighbour, Playa de Las Américas, whose boundaries have extended so far south that it's now hard to find the join between the two resorts.

The changing image of Playa de Las Américas has had an effect on Los Cristianos; the wide promenade has been extended, palm tree lined and landscaped and runs the entire length of the resort. Golden sand has been imported to coat the small coves that pepper the southern edge of the resort and new glass and chrome 'locales' are awaiting their upmarket retail tenants. In the race to go upmarket, Los Cristianos is reluctant to be left behind.

Beaches

In the centre of town, overlooking the port and its constant activity is the golden sand beach of Playa de Los Cristianos. Rows of umbrellas and sunbeds occupy the shoreline while at the back of the sand, beach volleyball courts are in near constant use. On the horizon, sailing boats, kayaks, canoes and pedalos tack their way across the water, fed by the schools and equipment hire businesses that hem the beach to the promenade.

Through the tunnel towards Las Américas is the vast expanse of Playa de Las Vistas, the south's best beach. Fine white sand has been imported, cleaned and pressed and lies in its Sunday best clothes in the shimmering heat haze. Two thirds of the beach is empty while the regimented rows of sunbathers crowd the water's edge.

Fishing boats - Los Cristianos

In deference to its origins, Los Cristianos is Tenerife's most disability friendly resort with beach terraces set aside for those with mobility problems and wheelchair users. Amphibian chairs and Red Cross staff are on hand to ensure that everyone can enjoy the seaside experience of a 'barrier-free paradise'.

Beyond the crazy golf and petanca courts, small, sandy coves dot their way from the centre of the resort to its southern end. The further you walk, the fewer people occupy them, until you reach Playa Callao where the sand is less disciplined, the vegetation has a mind of its own and you can find quiet corners and rocky platforms on which to be alone. Perfect for anyone who prefers their beaches a little less manicured and their tan a little more 'all over'.

Food

Amongst the glut of Italian restaurants and blackboards offering all day English breakfasts, you'll find a good selection of fish and seafood.

Right on the harbour, from **Casa Del Mar'**s panoramic terrace you can watch the fish being brought port-side as you tuck into an earlier catch (922 75 13 23; Explanade Del Muelle). Popular with locals is the no-frills **El Cine** (609 10 77 58; Juan Bariajo, 8) which is in an alley behind the chemist on the promenade. Service is seldom with a smile and you'll have to take whatever's on the menu but the fish is tasty and the bill is small.

On the border with Playa de Las Américas is the wonderful **Mesón Castellano** (922 79 63 05; Residencial El Camisón; *www.mesoncastellano.com*) where Serrano hams, salami and *salchichas* hang from the rafters and the menu is authentic Castilian and Canarian. Along San Telmo, a row of stylish eateries have terraces overlooking Playa de Las Vistas and tapas menus to keep you nibbling happily; amongst them **La Costa** (678 81 90 99; CC San Telmo, Local 4B; *www.lacosta-tenerife.net*) boasts 40 different dishes.

Veggies should head along to the **Olive Garden** (922 79 11 15; Paseo Marítimo, 5) where they'll find plenty of choice of good, tasty dishes but they'll have to fight for room alongside the carnivores as just about everyone is well catered for in this popular little corner.

Accommodation

The 2 star **Andreas Hotel** (922 79 00 12; Av. Valle Menéndez, 6; *www.hotelesreveron.com*) is a no-nonsense low budget option and well positioned for those spending the night before onward travel to one of the other islands.

On the site of Los Cristianos' first ever boarding house and still owned by the same family is the 4 star **Hotel Reverón Plaza** (922 75 71 20; C/ General Franco, 23; *www.hotelesreveron.com*). It's ideally situated for access to everything and has a quiet charm and style that in neighbouring Costa Adeje would have double the price tag. Speaking of which, the 4 star **Arona Gran Hotel** (922 75 06 78; Avda Juan Carlos, 1; *www.aronahotel.com*) at the most southerly edge of town is the place to go to be pampered.

Nightlife

Whilst the multitude of cabaret bars with their tribute acts will close at or around midnight sending the more mature Brits home to bed with the strains of 'Simply the Best' still ringing around their heads, the eclectic style bars of San Telmo will just be warming up about then and you can be anything *but* mature until the early hours.

Fiestas

The biggest festival of Los Cristianos' calendar is **Aguaviva** (*www.aguavivacanarias.com*). For three weeks in June, a line up of international bands including top name performers like Jamiroquai and Marc Anthony perform to a packed sports stadium while on the Conquistador beach (*technically* in Playa de Las Américas) there's free entrance to weekend parties featuring local and mainland bands and DJs; it's mini-Glasto by the sea.

Attractions

La Palma/La Gomera/El Hierro. Take advantage of the ferry portal to visit any of the other Western Canary Islands and discover somewhere that's under two hour's sailing and half a century away from Los Cristianos.

Monkey Park (*www.monkeypark.com*). Stock up on grapes and bananas from the breakfast buffet and head to this immensely popular little zoo where assorted primates will show no respect for personal space, eat your hair and then try the grapes.

Las Águilas Jungle Park (*www.aguilasjunglepark.com*). Act out your Indiana Jones fantasies over narrow suspension bridges in thick jungle with the cries of leopards and jaguars in the still air. Then watch eagles, vultures and falcons swoop to feed from the water and hope someone remembered to lock the reptile house.

Take to the warm seas that surround the resort to see whales and dolphins in their natural environment. Choose any trip that flies the yellow '*Barco Azul*' (it would have been *so* much more sensible to make the flag blue...) to ensure ethical practices and then prepare to be wowed.

MORE KETCHUP THAN SALSA

We set off home as the sun began its steady decline behind La Gomera, turning the mountains a glowing orange and laying huge shadows in the ravines. "Look over there," shouted Frank suddenly. We veered away from our coast-hugging route and headed further out to sea.

"What is it?" asked Joy.

"You'll see," he replied.

In the fading light we couldn't see anything unusual. Then all of a sudden, a shadow appeared under the water next to the boat. "Down there." Frank pointed.

The shadow broke the surface just six feet away from our boat, mirroring our speed and direction exactly.

"Dolphins," said Frank calmly. Another grey fin broke the surface a little further away, then another, and another. In seconds we were in the midst of a group of fifteen to twenty dolphins, all racing our boat.

Joy and I were mesmerised. They seemed to be playing with us, almost as curious about us as we were of them. One was almost close enough to touch but as I reached out, it sped forwards, leaping from the water ahead of us. Frank cut the engine and we drifted for a while as the dolphins submerged one by one and disappeared into the blue. The performance had ended, but the show had not.

Minutes had passed since we resumed our journey inland when a fish shot out of the water in front of us and flew inches above the waves before splashing down a hundred yards further on.

"Did you see that?" I said.

"Flying fish," said Frank, unimpressed. "You see loads of them out here." We approached the sparkling lights of the harbour in contemplative silence. I was completely absorbed by the sights and sounds; the playful creatures, the soporific swaying, the warm night breeze, the clinking of masts and ropes as we glided towards our mooring. I had temporarily forgotten our reason for being here. It was the first time since arriving that I felt like a traveller.

Even though at times it seemed this was an imported little Britain, full of patrons who thought that abroad was any sunny place where the locals couldn't talk properly, Frank's boat excursion and the indifferent behaviour of Lola and Pepe had provided a reminder that we were overseas.

Joe Cawley, *www.mytenerifeinfo.com*. Award-winning travel writer, copywriter & author of 'More Ketchup than Salsa'

Playa de Las Américas

Playa de Las Américas on Tenerife's sun kissed southern coast in the municipality of Arona has long held a reputation as a hedonistic holiday destination for under 25 year olds seeking boozy nights and lazy days on the beach and people who were looking for 'Blackpool in the sun'; however, the times they are a-changing.

Following its development from virtually uninhabitable badlands to bustling tourist resort in the 70s, Las Américas spread outwards, joining up with Los Cristianos on one side and into the neighbouring municipality of Adeje on the other. In recent years, realising that Las Américas had become synonymous with cheap, package holidays, Adeje re-branded their part of the resort as the upmarket 'Costa Adeje'. A smart strategy; it's not uncommon to hear people who would have baulked at the idea of staying in Las Américas remark: "Stay in Las Américas? Good God no, we're staying in Costa Adeje". Consequently the area once known as Playa de Las Américas seems to be shrinking.

> *"I think they've killed one part to cater for another part. In the old days you had 150 bars in the Veronicas stretch, and people came to the island to go to Veronicas. I think they could have handled the changes better."*
>
> **Joe Quaranta, owner of 'Bobby's Bar' in Veronicas, Playa de Las Américas, giving his thoughts on the south's new up-market image**
> (from an interview in Living Tenerife magazine - www.livingtenerife.com)

Las Américas has responded by attempting to re-invent itself. The 'beer and burger brigade' friendly bars still exist with their 'we sell normal food here' (whatever 'normal' is) proclamations etched on blackboards, but much of the resort has undergone a revamp. Stylish restaurants, trendy bars, five star hotels and shopping centres filled with designer brands have become the norm on the resort's wide, palm lined avenues. Nowadays Las Américas is a bright, clean modern resort which is becoming increasingly popular with nationalities other than the British, especially Eastern Europeans. The new image has given it an international ambience; although one which has more in common with Las Vegas than it does with the rest of Tenerife.

Beaches

Most of the resort's coastline is rocky with a few natural and man made rock pools. The only sandy beach is Playa del Camisón. Backed by a strip of palm trees, it's a picturesque, sheltered man made affair of golden-ish sand with sunbeds and pedalos.

A pleasant promenade running the length of the resort is accentuated by modern sculptures and benches which overlook the rocky Playa Honda and La Montañeta; an area with high waves which attracts surfers by the VW busload. It's a surprisingly un-touristy spot for a romantic dusk stroll.

Food

There are plenty of Italian, Indian, Chinese, Tex-Mex, Greek, Lebanese and 'International' (code for conservative cuisine) restaurants about the resort; although a shortage of traditional Canarian restaurants speaks volumes about Las Américas' lack of cultural identity. In recent years, the opening of cosmopolitan eateries with food as imaginative as their décor has added a chic flavour to the choice of cuisine on offer.

Unless eating at one of the Brit joints offering standard 'pub grub' around Starco and Veronicas, expect to pay substantially more for dining out than in many other areas.

Mamma Rosa (922 79 48 19; Apartamentos Colón 2) is a consistently reliable and popular, Italian restaurant which also dishes up 'creative cuisine'. Service is professional to the point of being stiff and can border on the pretentious, but the food is good - if you can put up with the live accordion music.

It's Argentinian, but **La Rana** (922 75 22 22; Parque Santiago V) is about as close as you'll get to Spanish cuisine in the main tourist area. The menu has a good selection of cheese, Iberian cuts and fish dishes, but steaks are what it's all about. If you're fussy about how your side of beef is cooked, opt for the one where they let you cook it yourself on a griddle at your table – unfortunately no discount for preparing your own dinner.

When sleek lines, chrome and furnishings which look as though they belong in an art gallery become too much, **El Gomero** (922 78 73 05; Avda. Antonio Dominguez) is a refreshingly unpretentious traditional Canarian joint with prices to match. Opposite the Magma Centre's architectural masterpiece, or muddle depending on personal taste, it's a popular haunt with taxi drivers and police, but hey, everybody's got to eat.

Accommodation

Do the full Las Vegas thing and book into one of the **Mare Nostrum's** five hotels (922 75 75 00; Avda Las Américas; *www.expogrupo.com*) in the upmarket end of the resort. With names like the **Marco Antonio**, **Julio Cesar** and **Cleopatra Palace**, the Roman theme matches that of the adjacent **Pirámide de Arona**. The pick of the hotels in the complex are the 5 star **Mediterranean Palace** and **Sir Anthony**.

Parque Santiago's (922 74 61 03; Avda Las Américas; *www.parquesantiago.com*) low-rise apartment complexes are consistently praised by families, couples, Uncle Tom Cobley and all. Their modern take on traditional Canarian architecture is attractive and apartments are conveniently located for beaches, bars and restaurants in whatever part of the resort takes your fancy.

Palacio de Congresos - Playa de Las Américas

Looking like an oversized, boldly coloured Mexican hacienda, **Hotel Villa Cortes** (922 75 77 00; Avda Rafael Puig; *www.europe-hotels.org*) delivers 5 star luxury with a great dollop of fun; you've got to love a place which has a 'catholic church on top of an ancient Mayan pyramid' in its grounds. Rooms are big and nicely decked out with wonderful balconies overlooking the sea. Even if you don't splash out on a room, the hotel's Chiringuito beach bar is *the* place to enjoy a cool cerveza at sunset.

Nightlife

A diverse, lively nocturnal scene is one of the reasons why visitors return year after year. No other resort can match the range of sports bars, fun pubs, drag and tribute acts, karaoke bars and clubs that are dotted about the neon lit streets; it's Tenerife's cabaret capital.

Younger visitors, whose holiday aspirations are to drink as much as they can without the aid of a stomach pump and try to strike up a 'holiday romance' in the process, populate 'the strip'; an area around the notorious C.C. Veronicas and C.C. Starco. This is the Tenerife of TV's 'Tenerife Uncovered' infamy; the place to party the night away at venues like the perennially popular **Lineker's Bar**, **Bobby's**, or **Wigan Pier** before heading to **Tramps** disco until dawn.

More mature night owls who enjoy a sing-a-long should head to the 'patch', near the Hotel Parque Santiago II and the Hotel Las Palmeras. There's a host of bars featuring comedians and live music; a place where time stands still and the likes of Billy Idol and Shirley Bassey sound-alikes still haven't passed their 'sell by' date.

If the idea of cabaret holds about as much appeal as a crucifix does to a vampire, there are some new 'style' bars around the C.C. Safari end of the resort which cater for the local 'in crowd'. **Buda**, **Harry's Cocktail Bar** and the **Magic Bar** should suit the more sophisticated set.

It might be kitsch, but a good way to check out what's going on is to take a horse drawn carriage tour of the resort at around €5 per person for 20 minutes.

Attractions

Carmen Mota Ballet - There isn't a better example of Las Américas' aspirations to be the Vegas of Europe than the row of bare breasted archers atop the columns of the mock Roman themed **Pirámide de Arona**, home to the lavish Carmen Mota Ballet (tickets €36). The building's so outrageously tacky that it's wonderful. The show itself is an enjoyable visual extravaganza, mixing Flamenco with opera and contemporary music (if you can call Dire Straits contemporary).

THE REALITY OF PLAYA DE LAS AMÉRICAS

How does the reality of Playa de las Américas compare to many people's perceptions?

To most people the very mention of Playa de las Américas conjures up images of all night bars and the very worst excesses. Virtually free from anything Canarian, row upon row of British Pubs, Fish and Chip shops and fast food outlets - this is a home from home for yob culture the place to come and party.

Well that might have been true several years ago but those in the know recognise that over the past few years Playa de las Américas has developed into a place that attracts families and middle aged couples, something for everybody including the most demanding of visitors, which is increasingly the target market.

You will quickly discover that a wide traffic free promenade runs along the full length of the resort. This begins at Los Cristianos and continues for several miles right through Playa de las Américas and on to La Caleta. One particular part of the promenade worth mentioning, is very sophisticated and should not be missed is around the Mare Nostrum complex which is filled with international restaurants, stylish cocktail bars. There are a large number of shopping complexes selling designer goods, perfume and jewellery stores. This lively, cosmopolitan resort with fantastic facilities and vibrant nightlife is for those looking for the ultimate sun, sea and sand destination and for those who want culture there is the Pirámides de Arona and the brand new Magma Centre which are the venues of top international entertainers.

Few would ever deny that Playa de las Américas is anything other than a modern purpose built tourist resort that boasts several sandy beaches, these days they are so well maintained you will never know they were man made, assorted water sports, countless shops and numerous restaurants. But in all honesty, it doesn't ever pretend to be anything else.

Playa de las América's appeal is that it attracts a more discerning visitor. It's Middle-England-On-Sea, the kind of folks who are more likely to pick up a broadsheet than tabloid; more likely to ask for a local wine than a pint of Stella. It isn't Nirvana; there is no town on this planet that can guarantee perfect functioning especially when several thousands of visitors move in each year to add to the normal population of inhabitants. But for the most part it feels civilised, laid back in a way that I couldn't find if I headed to many coastal resorts in Britain. That's the essence of Playa de las Américas long may it last. It comes with warts, but where doesn't?

Aguilas, TripAdvisor destination expert for Tenerife, *www.tripadvisor.com*

San Miguel de Abona

San Miguel sits at 600 metres above the coast and is one of the oldest towns in the south.

The TF28 on which it sits was built in the 1940s to connect the barren south to the populated north of the island and many of San Miguel's old buildings were demolished to make room for it. The new centre that grew around it is work-a-day, non-descript and indicative of what all of the south would look like today had the tourism boom of the 1970s not changed much of the face of the coast beyond Tenerife recognition.

Leave the main road to wander down streets that would test the stamina of a mountaineer, into the old town where the austere beauty of the Iglesia de San Miguel Arcángel marks the start of an old quarter where nicely renovated 18th and 19th century houses line narrow, cobbled streets with views over the volcanic landscape to the south coast.

San Miguel's best selling points are its semi-rural setting just a few kilometres but a million miles away from the busy coastal resorts so you still get the sunshine (albeit a degree cooler) along with fabulous accommodation and excellent restaurants.

Food

The town's former tobacco storage house, then Post Office and finally Cantina, **La Tasquita de Nino** (922 70 04 63; Calle Estanco; *www.latasquitadenino.com*) is the 18th century house in which the eponymous owner grew up and now serves beautiful tapas and traditional Canarian food; a delicious piece of local history.

Equally impressive culinary skills are exhibited at **La Pimienta Verde** (922 16 72 75; C/General del Sur, 39); a carnivore's Nirvana where the chops are MAN-sized and the steaks melt at the mere mention of a knife.

Accommodation

La Bodega Casa Rural (922 70 05 90; Bethencourt Alsonso, 4; *www.tenerife-labodega.com*) is an immaculately restored bodega which sits quietly behind its walls in the centre of town and conceals four stunning cottages set in glorious gardens. Also in the heart of town is the exquisite **Hotel Rural San Miguel** (922 16 79 22; C/Las Morales, 2; *www.hotelruralsanmiguel.com*) which is a restored 17th century mansion set around courtyards with its own thermal baths and atmospheric wine cellar.

The words 'spoilt' and 'choice' come to mind.

Nightlife

If a mock medieval castle, jousting and pulling chicken flesh from the bone with your bare hands while cheering on your Knight Errant rings your bell, the **Castillo San Miguel** (*www.castillosanmiguel.com*) will be right in your arena. If, on the other hand you'd prefer to spend the evening in Tenerife, pop downstairs in **La Bodega Vieja** to Jorge's 'Rincon del Ron' and express an interest in the wall of rum bottles; you'll be 'yo-ho-ho'-ing before the night's out.

San Miguel

Attractions

There's a small museum in **Casa de Dos Capitanes** at the town's El Calvario where they have displays of pottery and ceramics and lots of local history including a room dedicated to the use of camels for farming the south of the island.

A five minute drive or a pleasant hour's walk along an old Guanche trail takes you to the viewpoint of **La Centinela** from where you get widescreen vistas of the south airport and the resorts of Golf del Sur and El Médano set amidst arid, volcanic terrain.

Vilaflor

A town whose name stems from a Spanish captain's unrequited love; *'Vi la flor'* (I have seen the flower), a reference to a beautiful Guanche girl who the captain had encountered and immediately lost his heart to, in the pine forest surrounding the town. Unfortunately for the captain the girl didn't feel the same about him and hot footed it into the forest never to be seen again.

Vilaflor, lying at around 1500 metres above the south coast, is Spain's highest village and not the place to stay if a tan is your goal. At this height, clouds can, and do, sneak through the pines and fill the town's streets with a bone chilling mist. Most of the time the town nestles above the clouds; its temperate climate attracting visitors since Victorian times, when it was a popular spa destination. Nowadays, millions of tourists pass Vilaflor annually on their way to Mount Teide, but few venture onto its streets.

The heart of the town is around the Plaza and Iglesia de San Pedro, named after a humble goatherd born in Vilaflor who journeyed to Guatemala, founded the order of the Bethlehemites and subsequently achieved sainthood; the Canary Island's one and only saint.

Statues and references to Brother Pedro are all around the town's flower lined streets.

It's a pretty little community, but it doesn't take more than an hour to wander around and is probably going to appeal most to those wanting a quiet rural base for exploring the countryside.

Food

Vilaflor's southern approach is lined with potato terraces, so the *papas arrugadas* are particularly good here and its steaks are renowned, especially those in the restaurant at the **Las Lajas** picnic zone near the town. There are a selection of good restaurants in the town, including **El Rincon de Roberto** (922 70 90 35; Avda Hermano Pedro) with its slate walls and log fire, essential when the cloud invades; try the *degustación* of Canarian dishes – cheeses, *chistorias* (Canarian sausages) and *morcillas* (blood sausage with almonds and raisons).

Accommodation

Vilaflor's spa town past isn't completely consigned to history. The **Hotel Villalba** (922 70 99 31; Ctra San Roque; *www.hotelvillalba.com*) above the town looks the part for a hotel located in the middle of a pine forest and its range of spa treatments are a perfect antidote for aching limbs after a long trek. There are cheaper alternatives, perfectly pleasant rural pensions and hotels, in the centre of the town.

Attractions

In the town itself are some examples of traditional rural architecture, an old water mill, communal washhouse and a quirky little museum at the Hotel El Sombrerito. As you would expect from a town surrounded by mountains and forests, nature provides the best bits.

Just outside the town are a couple of oversized ancient pines. The path to some of the most unusual rock formations on the island, **Paisajes de Lunar**, begins further along the road. It's a three hour trek to reach, so those spa treatments might be welcome afterwards.

The night skies in Vilaflor are truly magical. A combination of the clarity of light, altitude and things that only an astronomer would understand make it possible to view stars that should be mathematically impossible to see from Tenerife.

WEST TENERIFE

The most westerly point of Tenerife is at Punto de Teno, reached via a road that cuts through the mountains and can only be accessed from the north coast, but it's the best spot to absorb one of the most spectacular views on Tenerife, the Teno Massif.

These ancient monoliths, one of the oldest parts of the island at 7 million years old, rise up from the sea providing a spectacular backdrop to the area's main resort, Los Gigantes. It's a relative newcomer to the western shores, barely a twinkle in developers' eyes until the late 1960s, unlike the remote hamlets characterised by traditional rural architecture which lie hidden in the folds of the mountains; the most famous of which is the beauty spot of Masca.

The coastal landscape, like the south, is dry and barren, enjoying the most sunshine hours and least rain on Tenerife. Until tourism made these features into the sun-seekers' Holy Grail, the only people who lived there were mainly fishermen in small communities at Alcalá, Playa de San Juan and Puerto de Santiago.

Nowadays the area has become popular with expatriates and visitors seeking a quieter alternative to the more lively resorts thirty minutes drive away to the south.

Head inland, past banana plantations and tomato crops and the scenery and the character of the west changes dramatically. At the wide plateau of Valle de Santiago, where agricultural practices have hardly changed in five centuries, two micro climates meet head on and you can virtually see the line where the low lying shrubs of the arid south meet the pine forests of the verdant north. The west of Tenerife provides a perfect illustration of the diversity of scenery, climate and culture which can be found in even one relatively small area of Tenerife.

Alcalá

The south and south west coast of Tenerife are regularly dismissed, somewhat inaccurately, as having been developed purely for the tourist market. Admittedly, there aren't many coastal communities which are uniquely Canarian, but the small fishing village of Alcalá is one of them.

A mishmash of streets are clustered around a small plaza and fishermen's jetty. Life, as with most Spanish communities, centres around the plaza. The village is populated by a mix of families from La Palma, La Gomera (in clear view across the water) and returning emigrants from Venezuela, lending it a unique Canarian/Latin American character.

"If Gomera's in sight, the weather's not right."
**Local saying about the weather on the south west coast
- clearly English as it wouldn't rhyme in Spanish**

Despite it being the most authentic village in the area, Alcalá was overlooked by visitors for decades, possibly because its rocky coastline is devoid of any decent sized beaches. The opening of a luxury hotel in 2008, built on the village's perimeter, brought it onto visitors' radar screens and businesses noticed an increase in trade within weeks of the hotel opening. Any concerns that the addition of a village sized hotel complex may change the nature of Alcalá are dismissed by locals like Domingo, a restaurant owner, whose uncomplicated philosophy illustrates the strength of culture that shapes the village.

"The hotel is there," he says pointing to the banana plantations at the western edge of town. "We are here." Simple as that.

Beaches

Some golden sand has been added to the tiny cove where the plaza meets the sea and a lifeguard has been employed to keep watch, but most locals sunbathe on the pleasant boardwalk which runs between the plaza and the small harbour.

Authentic fishing village of Alcalá

Food

Tenerife's fusion of Spanish, Canarian and South American culture is reflected in the choice of cuisine available at pavement cafes around the plaza. Choose from locally caught fish, tapas, traditional Canarian menus, pastries, or *arepas,* Venezuelan fried corn pancakes with a variety of fillings like *carne mechada* (spiced shredded meat). These are always served with an avocado and a lip-stinging piquant sauce. Arepas are common in Tenerife and are a delicious and cheap way of staving off hunger if you fancy a quick carb' hit.

Accommodation

A huge low-rise luxury hotel whose pale pumice exterior at least matches the tones of the surrounding terrain, the **Gran Melià Palacio de Isora** (922 86 90 00; *www.granmeliapalaciodeisora.com*) is located just beyond the western edge of the village. It's ideal for those who want to mix luxury with a soupçon of authentic culture. Much more suited to Alcalá's down-to-earth, workaday character is one of the pensions in the village itself.

Fiestas

The village pulls out all the stops for the celebrations in honour of the **Virgen del Carmen** around the 15th August. The plaza, all decked out in its fiesta finest, is ideally sized for getting into the thick of celebrations which feel as though they're taking place in some Latin American country. Live bands (salsa of course), fiesta queens and an offshore firework display liven up Alcalá's usually sedate nocturnal scene.

Los Gigantes

Los Gigantes lies on the sunny west coast in probably the most stunning location of all Tenerife's resorts. Its low-rise white buildings cluster at the foot of the 500 metre high, sheer face of the *Acantilados de Los Gigantes* (cliffs of the giants) from which the resort derives its name.

Developed in the 1960s, Los Gigantes is very much a British resort which many British ex-pats have chosen to make their home.

Unable to spread further west due to its precipitous position, it's managed to maintain a certain village feel about it; one where aerobic workouts for thighs and calves comes as standard every time you walk out of your front door.

Despite being hemmed in by the *Acantilados*, apartment blocks continue to be built into the cliff face, for which there really ought to be access via a ski lift, to meet the seemingly endless demand for residential and holiday accommodation in the resort.

Life tends to revolve around the pretty marina, the small square and the main street of Avenida Marítimo de Los Gigantes where shops, bars and restaurants cater almost exclusively to a British clientele. Without the clubs and late bars of the south, it's given a wide berth by the 18-30s and is better suited to families and those not given to 'mooning'.

Beaches

The only beach in Los Gigantes is the tiny, black sand Playa Los Guios behind the marina where you'll also find toilets.

Alongside the marina is the César Manrique designed complex of El Laguillo and further along the Avenida is the garden setting of Club Oasis. Both offer swimming pools, sunbathing and poolside snacks.

At the residential area of Crab Island there's a beautiful natural rock pool with a couple of conveniently flat rocks, nice for a late afternoon dip.

Food

Many restaurants and most bars provide standard pub grub but amongst the offerings are some surprising menus like **El Rincón de Juan Carlos** (922 86 80 40; Pasaje de Jacaranda, 2; *www.elrincondejuancarlos.es*) where the award winning chef presents creative cuisine that looks too good to eat but turns out to taste even better than it looks.

Accommodation

The only high rise building in the resort is also the only hotel; **Hotel Los Gigantes** (902 47 40 00; Avda Marítimo; *www.hotellosgigantes.com*), most of the resort's accommodation consists of apartments and aparthotels at varying heights from sea level to altitude.

Nightlife

Along Avenida Marítimo de Los Gigantes are a wide selection of bars and pubs screening Eastenders, hosting karaoke and offering cabaret, but don't expect to be crawling home as the lizards come out, they all close around the midnight hour.

Attractions

Sheltered from the Trade Winds by the *Acantilados*, the waters off Los Gigantes are deep, still and warm sustaining a host of microscopic marine life which attracts dolphins and whales. A large community of bottle-nosed dolphins live in these waters and many more cetaceans pass through on their migratory routes so that it's not uncommon to spot minke, sperm and even killer whales. Boats leave from the marina twice a day, amongst them are the flamboyant sailing vessel

'**The Flipper Uno**' (*www.flipperuno.com*) and the authentic former North Sea Crabber, the '**Katrin**' (*www.rmc-international.com/katrinenglish.htm*).

All boats flying the 'Barco Azul' flag operate within international guidelines which ensure ethical practices.

Masca

Even seasoned travellers will find it difficult not to gasp 'WOW' when they first set eyes on Masca. Tucked away in the folds of the 7 million year old Teno Massif in the west of the island, it occupies a breathtaking location and is often referred to as Tenerife's Shangri La. The approach, a series of switchbacks twisting and turning downwards through an incredible landscape, may appear nerve-racking for some; although there are plenty of *miradors* (viewpoints) en route at which to break up the rollercoaster descent and marvel at the scenery.

It's not only the vistas in Masca which are magical; tales of witchcraft and shape-changers abound in these parts. Once a rural farming community, narrow terraces still line the valley's slopes, tourism is now the main source of income. Daily, between 11.00am and 3.00pm, coaches and jeep safaris fill the car park above the hamlet, unloading their charges to wander its bougainvillea and palm lined cobbled walkways. The path between upper and lower Masca is steep and slippery and shoes with a decent tread are essential.

There's a view that the daily influx of tourists has diluted Masca's charm, I don't subscribe to this; tourism has brought prosperity and renewed life and the hamlet is immaculately maintained. Without tourism, Masca could have become just another abandoned rural community, much like the ones found on the neighbouring island of La Gomera, perfectly framed on the horizon.

Masca is simply a 'must see' for anyone visiting Tenerife. The time to catch it at its best is early morning and late afternoon, when it's devoid of the bulk of tourists. Escape the crowds at other times by making the short journey to adjoining Lomo de Masca which is equally picturesque.

Food

There's a surprising choice of attractive places to eat, all with fresh local produce from the surrounding valleys. **El Guanche** (922 86 34 24; C/El Lomito) serves delicious vegetarian meals; the goat's cheese from Teno is one of the best on the island. Try some homemade cactus lemonade at **El Fuente** (922 83 01 10) accompanied by breathtaking views. **Casa Blanky** occasionally has traditional musicians and is perfectly placed for weary walkers who have tackled the Masca Barranco.

Accommodation

Pensions and rural houses are available for rent for those who fancy experiencing the solitude of staying in such a remote community ... and maybe seeing a local metamorphose into a pig.

Nightlife

If you're sampling Masca the 24 hour experience, **Riquelme's** in Lomo de Masca is a bohemian bar with a pot-pourri of terraces and cosy corners in which to bask in glorious sunsets.

Attractions

A popular activity is hiking the **Masca Barranco**. Descend into an ancient landscape where narrow ravines close in overhead; a Jurassic Trek perhaps. Sensible walkers can arrange to be picked up by boat when they reach the bay three hours down the line (tickets from El Fuente); masochists can dip their toes in the water and make the return journey.

A **museum at Lomo de Masca** provides an interesting insight into village life pre-tourism.

Playa de la Arena

Geographically joined at the hip with Puerto de Santiago along Tenerife's western coast, it's difficult to tell where one ends and the other begins but, belonging to different municipalities, they reveal quite distinct personalities.

Playa de la Arena has benefited from investment in its infrastructure to create a clean, bright, family-friendly resort. The wide coastal promenade is lined with shops, bars and restaurants whose offerings reflect the predominantly British, and to a lesser extent German, visitors and ex-pats that choose to frequent it. Residential and holiday apartments climb up the hill behind the promenade, occupied from October to March by the 'swallows' who over-winter in this, the most benign of Tenerife's climates.

With new apartments springing up at an alarming rate along the main road at the back of the resort, it seems clear that Playa de la Arena is set to expand. But for now, the resort's main promenade retains a village feel where life is unhurried in the near constant sunshine.

Beaches

The island of La Gomera is the focal point on the horizon at one of the prettiest natural beaches on the island from which the resort derives its name; the blue flag Playa de la Arena. Backed by palm trees and bordered by cafes, restaurants and residential apartments, the small, black sand beach lies in a sheltered cove below the promenade. Nicely maintained toilets and shower blocks are worth the tiny fee for using them and make the beach a firm favourite with families.

Food

The resort isn't going to win any prizes for its varied gastronomic offerings but a wide choice of bars, restaurants and cafes offer largely uninspired menus to please mainly British palates. A cut above the rest are **Casa Pancho's** (922 86 13 23; Playa La Arena) on the beach where you can actually sample Spanish cuisine in the form of tapas, and **Maxime's** (922 86 24 15; Cueva del Polvo; *www.maximslosgigantes.com*) behind the Varadero end of the resort where French and Belgian cuisine comes at a price.

Accommodation

Much of the accommodation in the west is self-catering in good, value for money apartments. The best of the hotel offerings come from the two stables of Spring Hotels and the Barceló group.

Popular with Canarios at weekends, which means it must be good value for money, is the 4 star aparthotel **Barceló Varadero** (922 86 98 00; Avda La Gaviota, 1; *www.barcelovaradero.com*) at the southern edge of the resort. In the centre of the village, right opposite the beach, is the 4 star **Hotel Playa La Arena** (922 86 29 20; C/Lajial, 4; *www.springhoteles.com*) which no-one has a bad word to say about.

Nightlife

Nightlife is low key with bars offering karaoke and sports coverage. Those for whom Saturday night simply isn't complete without a tribute act or a comedian will have to put up with whatever cabaret their hotel is staging, or get a cab to Playa de Las Américas or Los Gigantes.

164

Playa de San Juan

One of a series of former fishing villages that dot the sunny south west coast of the island, Playa de San Juan is an up and coming resort where you can increasingly hear British voices enjoying its sea front restaurants.

Sheltered from the trade winds and facing the island of La Gomera, this stretch of coast enjoys the best of Tenerife's benign climate with little rainfall and abundant sunshine. Perfect for tourism; not so good for agriculture, which is why the area didn't develop until the late 1950s when wealthy emigrants to South America returned to their homeland and financed the building of wells and galleries to bring water to the coast.

Retaining less of a traditional feel than its nearest neighbour Alcalá, the tone of Playa de San Juan's development is being set by its picturesque marina and the deluxe 5 star Abama Hotel which sits, mercifully partially obscured, on the headland above the village. A palm tree lined boardwalk runs the length of the promenade, restaurants are stylishly glass and chrome and apartments with sunset views over La Gomera sell for premium prices.

Beaches

Until recently, a small black sand beach in between the town and the marina was the most popular spot for sunbathers while beyond the brightly coloured fishing boats, a long pebble beach was little used. Now, the black pebble beach has miraculously turned into golden sand (well more two-tone really with the black sand re-emerging at the water's edge) stretching all the way round the headland to the restored lime kiln. Backed by changing rooms, watched over by a lifeguard and just a step from boardwalk cafes, it's proving to be a popular development.

165

Food

As you'd expect, fresh fish is the usual 'menu del dia' and there are plenty of restaurants to choose from. But for something really special, try the contemporary and ultra stylish **Marlin** (922 83 23 65; C/Artes de Mar, 1; *www.marlin-restaurante.com*) opposite the pier; rice, fish and Galician seafood are the specialities and the terrace is a great place to people watch by day and a romantic rendezvous by night.

Accommodation

The dusky pink (yes, pink) coloured building the size of a small village on the headland above Playa de San Juan is the 5 star **Abama Resort** (922 12 60 00; C/General; *www.abamahotelresort.com*) Comfortable and facility-rich it may be, with 10 restaurants, eight pools and an 18 hole golf course, but in keeping with the area it certainly isn't.

By contrast, **Carla's Apartments** (922 86 59 67; Avenida Emigrante, 6*)* at the start of the marina are bright, spacious and have the added bonus of ringside sunset views over La Gomera and the dulcería downstairs for breakfast.

Puerto de Santiago

As the road continues west from Playa de la Arena into Puerto de Santiago you begin to notice slight differences; the restaurants become amusement arcades, buildings need a new coat of paint and '*Se Aquiler*' and '*Se Vende*' signs decorate windows.

Beyond a narrow, pedestrian-unfriendly turn in the road, steps fall steeply to the heart of this fishing village; a small harbour where fishing boats and a tiny ermita sit alongside the quay.

At its westerly edge the resort drops down to a headland where the Barceló Santiago hotel has spawned a small centre brimming with bars, restaurants, supermarkets and souvenir shops.

But recent investment in a large four star hotel high above the resort has signalled a change in its fortunes; a pretty coastal walkway has been constructed which runs from the harbour to the most westerly headland on one side and through manicured gardens below the plaza and along the coast to Playa de la Arena on the other.

With Puerto de Santiago, you get the feeling it's fair to say "watch this space".

Beaches

There are plans underway to re-develop the coast below the plaza, but for the moment the resort's only offering is a black sand beach the size of a postage stamp bordering the harbour. Further westwards below the walkway, low tide reveals beautiful rock pools, perfect for snorkelling and swimming.

Food

Around the harbour area, the somewhat tatty exteriors of restaurants conceal expansive terraces overlooking La Gomera where the food is unpretentious and menus are locally focused.

Around the Barceló Santiago a clutch of bars, restaurants and cafes cater to mainly British clientele with few gastronomic exceptions to write home about.

Accommodation

The stylish 4 star **Barceló Santiago** (922 86 09 12; La Hondura, 8; *www.barcelosantiago.com*) sits on a promontory with awesome views over the cliffs of Los Gigantes, best enjoyed from its elegant sun terrace.

Spring Hotel's latest offering is the 4 star **Costa Los Gigantes** (922 86 72 72; C/Juan Manuel Capdevielle 8;

167

www.costalosgigantes.com) which, despite its name, is actually in Puerto de Santiago, perched with the Gods high above the resort. All glass, chrome and vertigo, its clean lines and minimalist chic provide all inclusive to those who daren't leave the hotel for fear of having to do the return slog on foot.

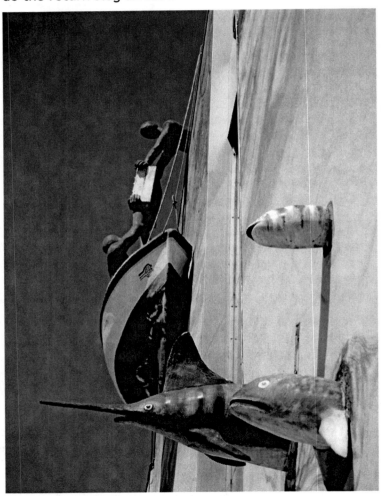

Bernard Romain's sculpture at **Museo del Pescador**

Nightlife

The bars around Barceló Santiago offer live music and tribute acts most nights of the week.

Attractions

Easy to miss as you keep your eyes on the narrow 'S' bend that centres Puerto de Santiago, is the sea blue wall of the **Museo del Pescador** (*www.museodelpescador.com*) where Bernard Romain's amazing 3D canvas has fishermen unloading their catch onto the quayside and the tails and heads of swordfish and sharks disappearing into and emerging from the wall. A full calendar of exhibitions showcases local and international artists as well as new talent in this unsung gem of a museum.

Santiago del Teide

Santiago del Teide sits 1000 metres above sea level in the centre of the valley of the same name. It's best known as the place where the 'white knuckle ride' drive to Masca begins. The town spans two microclimates; one side is semi arid, save for almond trees which fill the valley with delicate pink blossom in January and February. On the other, pine trees line the hillsides. Its position meant that it wasn't considered prize land for conquering noblemen following the conquest, so it was given over to the Guanche, resulting in a strong bloodline whose influences are still evident today.

The town has a different character than Tenerife's other hill towns; its main street dissects whitewashed cottages with colour wash emerald windows and door frames, some of which have been livened up by local artist, Bernard Romain's enchanting depiction of the eight main Canary Islands (that's not a mistake; legendary San Borondón is included). It feels more like a Mexican pueblo; cactus plants which line flat roofs and women wearing wide brimmed straw hats only serve to enhance this notion. It is literally a one-horse town; except Santiago's horse, which stands outside a bodega on the main road, isn't real.

Plots surrounding the town are filled with rows of gnarled vines and potato plants, all still cultivated by hand. In spring, nature goes all Van Gogh and the valley is covered in a sea of scarlet poppies, lavender and crimson tabaiba. However nature hasn't always been kind to Santiago. In 1909 Mount Chinyero blew its top (the last eruption on Tenerife) and streams of lava reached to the front doors of the valley's villages. A disaster was averted only, so folklore has it, by divine intervention; images of Santa Ana, Christ and the Virgen Mary were carried to the edge of the lava flow...and it stopped. In 2008 furious forest fires swept to within feet of the valley's communities.

It's a good location for lacing up the hiking boots and heading into the great outdoors. Goat trails, a legacy from Guanche times, crisscross the valley traversing neat terraces, volcanic landscapes and pine forests.

Food

As with all farming country, hearty peasant stews and broths figure highly on restaurant menus; even straightforward sounding *carne con papas* (meat and potatoes) is served up as a type of broth with garlic and chillies. **Chinyero Bodego** (922 86 40 40; Avda General Franco), the place with the horse, and the agricultural market next door (open Saturday and Sunday) are good places to pick up some local wines and goodies and **Bar Fleytas** (922 83 01 10; Ctra General Erjos, 53), starting point for many walking routes, has scrumptious home made *almendrados* (almond cakes).

Attractions

The valley's been a centre for pottery making since pre-conquest. Pick up some Guanche inspired earthenware at **Cha Domitila**, a charming little pottery workshop and museum in nearby Arguayo.

Casa El Patio, behind the Iglesia de San Fernando, wouldn't look out of place plonked in a field in Tuscany. It's the planned location of the town's agricultural museum, but until it actually opens to the public, visitors have to make do with enjoying its aesthetic pleasures from a distance.

Las Cañadas

To the original inhabitants of Tenerife, the Guanche, it was the place where the earth held up the sky; to Columbus' crew of the *Santa Maria* in 1492, it was a bad omen, erupting as they passed it, but to 3.5 million people every year, Mount Teide represents the literal and symbolic highlight of their holiday.

An icon, not only of Tenerife but of the whole archipelago, Mount Teide stands in a 16 kilometre wide crater known as Las Cañadas del Teide where, at 3718 metres above sea level, it's Spain's highest mountain and Europe's highest volcano.

Las Cañadas is a surreal landscape of russet coloured lava flows, orange volcanic cones, shiny black obsidian rivers, extraordinary rock formations standing proud above white pumice fields and towering crater walls beneath an iridescent blue sky.

In winter snow covers the peak and lies in compacted ice on the crater floor and in spring Las Cañadas blossoms into a kaleidoscope of colour as the Teide violet, the white broom and the two metre high crimson peaks of the Tajinaste spikes come into flower.

Food

In the **Parador** a self-service style cafeteria and a large restaurant charge prices that have you wondering why the staff aren't wearing stockings over their faces. Much better value and even more spectacular views from the restaurant and bar/cafeteria of the cable car station which has a good range of offerings and the distinction of being Spain's highest eating establishment.

Accommodation

In a stunning setting at the base of the crater wall is Tenerife's only **Parador** (922 38 64 15; *www.paradores-spain.com/spain/pcanadesteide.html*). Packed by day with visitors using the cafeteria and the toilets, at night you get the crater and the starry heavens all to yourself.

Attractions

Every tour company on the island offers the Teide experience which consists of taking the **Cable Car** to a height of 3555 metres above sea level; a rise of 1200 metres in eight minutes. It's not for vertigo sufferers but the rewards are breathtaking; views over the crater of Pico Viejo and Gran Canaria, La Palma, La Gomera and El Hierro floating on the horizon.

Second stop on the tour is the **Roques de García**; spectacular volcanic dykes from which the wind has eroded the rock, leaving towering sculptures of solid magma that defy gravity by being skinny at the base and wide at the top.

Leave the crowds behind and head out on foot to explore this extraordinary landscape. Well signposted trails matrix the Cañadas and you can pick up a guide at the Visitor Centre at Portillo. For the ultimate challenge, set off from the base of Montaña Blanca to hike to Teide's summit for which you'll need a permit.

It's a gruelling four and a half hour contest of you vs. altitude and fatigue to get to the Altavista Refuge and another hour and a half from there to the peak, but that's child's play compared to the effort required to get a permit.

Avoid the bureaucracy by staying overnight at the refuge and reaching the peak for sunrise for which you don't need a permit. Home comforts at the refuge run to a bunk bed, a table on which to rest your elbows, two toilets between 50 people and unless the temperature drops to minus seven or more, no heating.

Mount Teide - Las Cañadas

Essential Travel Information

EMERGENCY TELEPHONE NUMBERS

There's one number to rule them all. Call 112 for any emergency; ambulance, police and fire services or sea and mountain rescue. It makes life very easy, especially as operators speak English and German as well as Spanish.

CRIME

Tenerife is still a relatively crime free island, although like anywhere there are instances of petty theft, especially in the main southern tourist areas where people are more relaxed and a little less vigilant than when at home. Areas with high Canarian populations generally experience fewer problems.

The best approach to avoid becoming a victim is to apply common sense. Don't leave valuables on display in cars, or handbags unattended in bars, or on the beach.

One of the nice qualities about Tenerife is that it's generally a safe place for women travelling on their own. Across most of the island, young girls walk home alone on dark streets or on country roads in the early hours without any fear of harassment. However, once again this doesn't necessarily apply in areas which have a predominantly transient population.

DRIVING

Tinerfeños are not the best drivers in the world; they suffer from a lack of concentration combined with an apparent lack of understanding of the rules of the road, so minor bumps are commonplace. In fact they're almost expected. When I took my car in for its first service, the mechanic was sceptical that I ever took it on the road because it didn't have a dent in it.

Being armed with the knowledge that drivers around you are likely to do the unexpected is half the battle won, particularly if you're doing what many of your fellow drivers aren't...concentrating. Despite the unpredictability of some Tinerfeño road users, confident drivers shouldn't experience any problems and on the whole should find Tenerife's country roads a pleasure to drive on.

Some visitors are surprised to return to where they parked their car to find that it's been towed away; usually because it was parked illegally. There's a simple solution to avoid this; don't behave any differently than you would in your own country. It might look as though the locals get away with double parking, parking on pedestrian crossings and any number of minor traffic offences...they don't. Car pounds are full of vehicles with registrations which begin with 'TF'.

Speed traps have become commonplace in Tenerife, so drive within the limits, not always easy as these can fluctuate wildly over short distances, otherwise you could be hit with a €100 fine.

Local wags claim that Guardia Civil presence on the roads increases when a fiesta is due and they need to boost their fiesta funds.

HEALTH

As a province of Spain, Tenerife has a very good public health service which is free for anyone who pays Spanish national insurance contributions, or has a European Health Insurance Card (EHIC). There are two public hospitals on Tenerife; in La Laguna (Urb Ofra; 922 67 80 00) and Candelaria (C/Periodista Ernesto Salcedo; 922 50 01 01). A third is being built near Los Cristianos, but it's a case of don't hold your breath waiting for completion. The only hospitals in the south of the island are private ones; however most towns have public medical centres. If you can't speak Spanish, some centres won't deal with you unless you're accompanied by a translator.

Using the public health service can involve long waiting periods, whereas having private medical insurance will mean any health issues are dealt with quickly, professionally and efficiently; private hospitals on Tenerife are excellent and staff speak English and German as well as Spanish. There are private hospitals (*www.hospiten.com*) in Santa Cruz, Puerto de la Cruz and Playa de Las Américas.

Whilst the EHIC entitles you to free health care, it doesn't cover the cost of repatriation. In the case of a serious health issue private insurance is essential to cover the cost of transport back to your home country.

Anyone who finds themselves with a minor ailment, should forget queuing at a medical centre and head to the nearest *farmacia*. Pharmacies are great places for seeking advice relating to minor ailments and can prevent unnecessary visits to the GP.

SHOPPING

Best Buys

With tax free status, the Canary Islands are a great place to pick up cheap cigarettes, booze, perfume and cameras. Every decent sized town and resort has a proliferation of camera and perfume shops and every supermarket offers a large selection of cigarettes and brand name and local spirits. In some coastal resorts of the south, it's not unusual to see small supermarkets with four aisles of booze and one of everything else.

Good filter coffee is very good value, although some of the packaging would cause outrage in today's politically correct Britain, and items such as olive oil and saffron can be bought for a fraction of UK prices.

Food

The north of the island is served by a vast network of supermarkets where, depending on the strength of the pound to the euro, the weekly shopping bill will come in at around a third cheaper than in the UK. Even the smallest towns will have at least one, and often two or three of the main supermarket chains of Mercadona, Hyper Trebol, HyperDino and Altesa; each of whom overwhelms with aisles full of yoghurts, olives, biscuits and Serrano hams as well as fruit and vegetables and a fresh fish counter where a bewildering range of sea creatures are cleaned and gutted to order. Most also have their own butchery and bakery.

The island's hypermarkets are Al Campo (Santa Cruz, La Laguna, La Orotava) and Carrefour (Santa Cruz) where you can buy everything from beds to beans.

In the southern resorts of the island the supermarkets tend only to cater for the basic needs of holidaymakers and many ex-pats make a weekly trip to Las Chafiras to the larger supermarkets.

Top of Tenerife's local produce is honey; 15 types are produced from the island's flowers, including the tajinaste where mobile hives are taken into the crater in spring so that the bees can collect the pollen. Look out for the 'Miel de Tenerife' label. Equally good is the La Gomera produced Miel de Palma; a rich, dark, toffee flavoured natural honey produced from palm sap. It's delicious in Greek yoghurt, drizzled over smoked goats' cheese, porridge or ice cream or added to dressings. And while on the subject of goats' cheese, Arico smoked is one of the world's top twelve cheeses and should make it onto every visitor's shopping list.

Clothes

Large commercial centres have Spanish outlets such as Women's Secret, Punta Roma and Zara as well as its sister shops Stradivarius and Bershka. In Playa de Las Américas and Costa Adeje, upmarket centres like Safari and Plaza Del Duque are brimming with brand name outlets aimed at the wallets and purses of the 'more discerning' visitor that the resorts are now attracting.

Santa Cruz has one of Europe's largest open air shopping zones and several commercial centres with Spanish and UK high street favourites as well as a good selection of independents. The Spanish version of Selfridges; Cortes Inglés is also in the capital.

For shoes, look out for the cheap and cheerful Carolina Boix and the fabulously stylish but more expensive Pécas.

Resources

MAGAZINES AND NEWSPAPERS

Diario de Avisos, El Día, La Opinión - Tenerife's three main daily Spanish language newspapers. Good for practising your Spanish and finding out what's happening on Tenerife at the same time.

Hoy and Today - Handy little free monthly mag in Spanish and English with listings of concerts, theatre performances, exhibitions, nightlife, restaurants. It also has a gay friendly section.

Island Connections - A long established fortnightly English language newspaper with news reports about all the Canary Islands, but the focus is mainly on Tenerife.

Lagenda - Free monthly cultural agenda in Spanish (listings are easy to understand even if your grasp of Spanish is nil), with info on live music, clubs and concerts on Tenerife. A great guide for night owls who want to experience the night scene which exists outside of the purpose built resorts.

Living Tenerife - The number one free monthly English language lifestyle magazine on Tenerife with location reports, articles about the Tenerife outside the tourist resorts, restaurant and concert reviews, fashion and lifestyle tips.

Tenerife News - Tenerife's other main English language newspaper, also issued fortnightly, which covers much the same ground as Island Connections as well as including some international news.

Western Sun - Fortnightly English language newspaper mainly covering news and events in the south west of Tenerife.

BOOKS

Native Flora of the Canary Islands; Miguel Ángel Cabrera Pérez: ISBN: 84-241-3555-5

Exotic Flora of the Canary Islands: Juan Alberto Rodríguez Pérez: ISBN: 84-241-3552-0

There are a lot of different flowers and plants on Tenerife and these two illustrated books are crucial tools for identifying what most of them are. Both are handy sized for fitting into the rucksack.

More ketchup than Salsa: Joe Cawley; ISBN: 978-1840245011

A highly amusing account of the ups and downs of running a bar in the south of Tenerife; populated with larger than life characters that will be recognisable to anyone who's spent any time in any purpose built resort which caters for the Brits.

Real Tenerife Island Drives: Andrea & Jack Montgomery: ISBN: 978-8461126583

The essential travel guide for visitors hiring a car on Tenerife who want to discover the best of the island's scenery and its hidden corners. Easy to follow instructions make map reading a thing of the past.

Tenerife Lifeline: Leslie Beeson: ISBN: 978-8461265510

A bible for anyone moving to Tenerife on a permanent basis; full of detailed and indispensable information about all aspects of setting up home and working on Tenerife. Includes sections on buying property, tax, setting up a business and much, much more.

Tenerife and the Western Canary Islands: ISBN: 979-0887297809

Excellently written book which really gets under the skin of Tenerife and its past. The guidebook aspect is minimal, but for background, history and an insight into what makes Tenerife tick, it's unmatched.

WEBSITES

Canary Green: *www.canarygreen.net*
In environmentally friendly terms, Tenerife and the Canary Islands have a bit of catching up to do; this 'green' site is full of interesting information about what the island is doing to redress the balance.

Colin Kirby: *www.colinkirby.com*
Informative and witty all round blog about the latest goings on in Tenerife; especially of interest to anyone who wants to find out about sporting events on the island.

Cyberhiker: *www.cyberhiker.co.uk*
The best way to discover Tenerife's great outdoors is on foot. Gary Rosson's site is passionate about Tenerife as a walking holiday destination and ideal for arranging tailor made walking holidays.

Etenerife: *www.etenerife.com*
An excellent online resource for visitors and residents alike with information covering a whole range of subjects; particularly good for anyone planning on bringing up children on Tenerife.

Living Beneath the Volcano:
http://tenerifevirgins.wordpress.com
An irreverent blog about the fun and frustrations that are part and parcel of living in the north of Tenerife and coming to terms with another culture's quirks.

Living Tenerife: *www.livingtenerife.com*
Property for sale, fashion, travel features, interviews and more in Tenerife's number one lifestyle website.

My Tenerife Info: *www.mytenerifeinfo.com*
Information website by award winning author Joe Cawley which means you get Joe's inimitable take on a whole host of things to do and see on Tenerife including, reviews of restaurants, nightlife and hotels.

Puntoinfo: *www.todotenerife.es*
Official Canary Council website in different languages with absolutely loads of information on all aspects of Tenerife. Excellent resource tool, although the information on some Spanish pages is more comprehensive than those on the equivalent English ones.

Real Tenerife Island Drives: *www.realtenerifeislanddrives.com*
Website aimed at the more adventurous travellers, with information about the Tenerife which exists beyond the tourist brochures, including in-depth low downs on the island's main fiestas. Also includes an independent guide to car hire companies on Tenerife.

Secret Tenerife: *www.secret-tenerife.com*
The most detailed English language website on the island with an overwhelming amount of information about everything that's going on in Tenerife, including political shenanigans and the reality of rural living. Amusingly written, with the great and the good of Tenerife often finding themselves at the receiving end of author, Pamela Heywood's sharp wit.

Sorted Sites: *www.sortedsites.com*
The best web design and IT business solutions company on Tenerife. Should be the first stop for anyone who wants a web presence on Tenerife.

Tenerife Forum: *www.tenerifeforum.com*
A friendly online community which focuses mainly on southern, and therefore British, areas and themes.

However, the detailed advice and information on a range of topics is very useful for anyone thinking of spending time anywhere on Tenerife

Tenerife Tattle: *http://tenerife-tattle.blogspot.com*
Amusing blog about life in Tenerife's south and the challenges of bringing up children in a different culture.

Tenerife Times: *www.tenerifetimes.com*
Information about Tenerife with content supplied mainly by residents.

Tenerife - Training: *www.tenerife-training.net*
Guided cycle tours on Tenerife; great site for anyone interested on exploring Tenerife's countryside on two wheels and without an engine.

MORE LINKS

A complete and up-to-date list of web links to estate agents, language learning resources, hotels, travel companies and other useful contacts for visitors and investors in Tenerife can be found at: *www.nativespain.com*

About Andrea & Jack

In 2003 Jack and Andrea Montgomery stepped off the corporate ladder, jettisoned financial security and swapped life in a Manchester suburb for the sunshine and fiestas of Tenerife. Based in the north of the island, they now live amidst banana plantations at the foot of Europe's largest volcano; Mount Teide.

In order to make a 'livi' (a 'livi' is almost a living), they exchanged writing about North West England's disadvantaged groups and skills shortages for photographing and writing articles about Tenerife's rich heritage, its picturesque villages and dramatic coastlines. A lucky break in the form of a case of mistaken identity introduced them to *Living Tenerife's* editor and they began submitting regular features to the magazine's glossy pages.

Their work involves travelling the island to parts that visitors and even most residents never see, trekking along goat trails in the mountains, treading the streets of every town and village, revelling at fiestas until dawn (all in the name of research) and spending endless hours poring over books and hundreds of English and Spanish language websites and translating reams of sleep inducing Spanish text.

What Jack and Andrea have discovered is an island rich and diverse in landscape, culture, history and tradition, great chunks of which are entirely overlooked by information sources, tour groups and even the most reputable travel guides.

Armed with all this first hand knowledge and experience they have written 'Going Native in Tenerife' so that others may discover the island's hidden delights.

Passionate about promoting the Tenerife that exists beyond the holiday brochures, they're now authors, feature writers, corporate bloggers and photographers for magazines and websites and they reckon there are still parts of their beautiful adopted homeland waiting to be discovered...on foot.

REAL TENERIFE ISLAND DRIVES

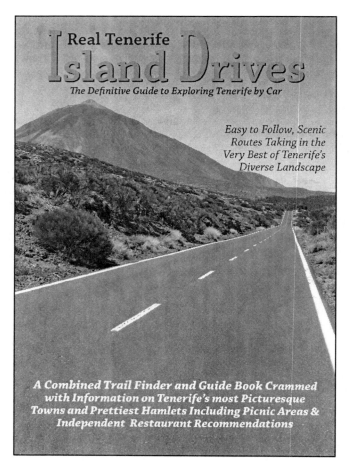

Packed with information, anecdotes and stunning photographs,
Island Drives makes sure you'll get the most from your car hire
and holiday in Tenerife. Explore a vibrant, fascinating and
friendly island rich in natural beauty, history and culture.
Discover the Tenerife that many visitors never see...

www.realtenerifeislanddrives.com

"What the guidebooks failed to tell you about living, working and investing in Spain."

NativeSpain.com

Spain

2008 the expat survival guide

Yolanda Solo

"if you live in Spain you need this book"

www.nativespain.com

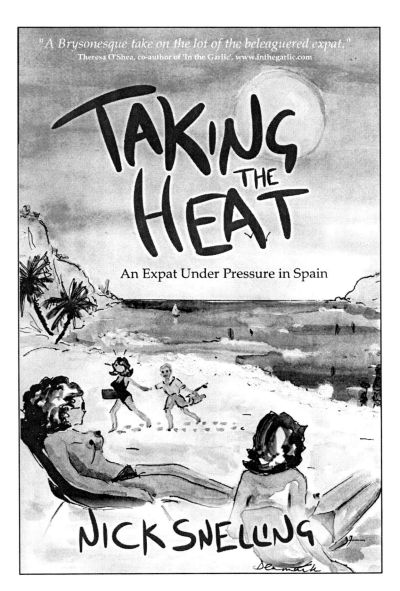

"A Brysonesque take on the lot of the beleaguered expat."
Theresa O'Shea, co-author of 'In the Garlic', www.inthegarlic.com

TAKING THE HEAT

An Expat Under Pressure in Spain

NICK SNELLING

www.nativespain.com

NativeSpain.com

Going Native in
Catalonia

Simon Harris

the essential guidebook for the inquisitive explorer

www.nativespain.com